CHINESE MADE EASY

Spoken Chinese In Hundred Lessons

Second Edition

Syed Hasan Javed

Paramount Books (Pvt.) Limited

Karachi | Lahore | Islamabad | Faisalabad | Peshawar | Abbottabad | Hyderabad

Chinese Made Easy

by

Syed Hasan Javed

First Edition 2012

Second Edition.................2014

Paramount Books (Pvt.) Limited

152/O, Block-2, P.E.C.H.S., Karachi-75400, Pakistan

Tel: 34310030, Fax: 34553772, E-mail: paramount@cyber.net.pk

Website: www.paramountbooks.com.pk

ISBN: 978-969-494-976-5

Printed in Pakistan

This book is dedicated to the everlasting friendship between Pakistan and the Peoples' Republic of China

“Great acts are made up of small deeds.”

Lao Tzu 604-531 BC , the founder of Taoism

The Author

Ancient Silk Route Caravan from China

arriving in Pakistan

(By: Ayesha Hasan Javed)

Yin-Yang creates Balance and Harmony

ین یانگ کا امتزاج ــــــــ توازن اور ہم آہنگی

Contents

Preface

The successful launching of the First Edition of the 'Chinese made easy' reminded me of what the ancient Chinese military strategist Sun Tzu had said that "opportunities multiply when they are seized". Chinese sage Confucius had stated that 'the first step in a 1000 kilometer journey', is most important step. We are not only witnessing the dawn of a new global era but are on the threshold of new history. Pakistan has to prepare well for it. The learning of Chinese language will help us access the awesome and enormously rich Chinese soft power value system and cultural heritage without which China would not have achieved its quantum economic and social progress. I would consider my book as indeed the first step of the 1000 kilometer journey. Every small step however counts.

Knowing a foreign language, works wonders as an important means of soft power. Given the strong linkages and historical relationships between Pakistan and China, the opportunities in our cooperation can only be fully harnessed, if we know languages of each other's. Knowledge of Chinese language will make us 'culturally interoperable' and in a better position to understand the culture, history, philosophy, ethics, business and societal thought processes.

My book provides smart and innovative multi-medium tools, to overcome the tone and sound difficulties in learning of Chinese language. My book has been well-received in Beijing, where I launched it at the Department of South Asian Studies, Beijing University on 10 September 2012 and in Karachi and Islamabad from 5-12 October, 2012.Some School Systems, teaching institutions and boards of Education are also considering to include it as the text for Conversational Chinese lessons. For the Chinese, my book provides the easiest and the shortest medium to learning Simplified Conversational Urdu. I hope that my humble efforts will be able to bring together the future generations of Pakistanis and Chinese, in shaping their destiny together.

Acknowledgment

'The proof of the pudding is in eating', goes the English saying. The proof of the popularity of any book is in its first few weeks of publication. This is what has happened with this humble work of mine. The book had a built in demand for itself with the result that immediately on its launch, the book started running out of stock in the famous book stores with frantic calls and e mails to the author on where it could be available. The younger generation of Pakistan like the rest of the world, is not only keen to learn the Chinese language but also become a part of the economic success story of China. I knew for long the thirst Pakistanis had for learning Chinese language. The difficulties a beginner faces in learning Chinese language, was also as fresh in my mind as it was when I began my first lessons in September 1980 at the then Beijing Languages Institute. I was therefore not at all surprised by the spontaneous reception that 'Chinese Made Easy' received at the various launching events organized by the eminent Universities and Institutions in Pakistan and abroad.

The book 'Chinese Made Easy' is on its way to become the most popular Chinese language learners' book, travel companion, business directory and an official's reference book for Pakistanis and Chinese alike. I chose to launch 'Chinese Made Easy' during my visit to Beijing to attend the 50th Anniversary Celebrations of Beijing Languages University (formerly Beijing Institute of Languages) at their invitation from September 8 -11, 2012 being an alumnus of the esteemed institution. My old friend, Prof Tang Mangsheng, invited me to launch 'Chinese Made Easy' at the Department of South Asian Studies, Beijing University, on September 10, 2012. The event was attended by Former Ambassador Lu Shu Lin, Former Ambassador Wei Weikang, former diplomats, scholars, teachers and students. The book was termed as a 'historic contribution' that would enhance people to people contacts and promote even closer friendship and cooperation between the two countries. One advantage of the book is its feature of linguistic "inter-operability", as a facilitator for the learning of simplified Urdu conversation for the Chinese people and other foreigners. The English sub-texts are meant to be force multiplier. This book will help the younger generation of Pakistanis and Chinese to shape their destinies together.

The book has been launched at the Institute of Business Administration, Karachi; NUST Business School, Islamabad; Roots School System's Chinese Language Department; Taxila Institute of Asian Civilization at Quaid e Azam University and Faculty of Arts, University of Karachi. I have also received requests for the book's launching from a dozen other universities / Associations in Pakistan and abroad.

From the feedback received, the book's useful features are its multi-medium tools, methodical presentation and utilitarian value. I am thankful to my friend, Mr. Lu Shui Lin, former head of Urdu Department China Radio International, who provided a thorough review and feedback on the content. I also thank my brother-in-law, Dr. Saiyid Fazal Wahid, who provided his useful input on paraphrasing the 'pearls of wisdom'. I am grateful to Paramount Publishers who made detailed arrangements for making available copies during the launching of the book .My special gratitude goes to Heads of the esteemed institutions mentioned above including Dr. Muhammad Qaiser Vice Chancellor and Professor Dr. Nasiruddin Khan Registrar, University of Karachi, Dr, Masoom Yaseenzai, Vice Chancellor, Professor Dr. Ashraf Ali Khan Director and Dr. Ghani Ur Rehman Deputy Director of the Taxila Institute of the Asian Civilization, Quaid- e- Azam University , Lt. General (Retired) Engineer Muhammad Asghar and Professor Dr. Ashfaque Hasan Khan, Dean NUST Business School, Dr. Ishrat Hussain, Rector and Captain(Retired)AhmadZaheer Registrar IBA,Institute of Business Administration Karachi, and Mr. Faisal Mushtaque Director of the Roots School System Islamabad for their cooperation and generosity in launching the book. Once again, I thank my Assistant Mr. Attique Tabasam and Secretary Ms Tham Sok Yin Eileen for their continued help. I am also grateful to all the readers and well-wishers whose words of appreciation continue to inspire and humble me.

Finally, my profound gratitude is for my Beijing-born daughter, Javeriya Hasan, who had typed the original manuscript before the print version was prepared, for again lending her precious time to contribute to this edition. I am also grateful to my wife, Mrs. Shahnaz Javed and my three younger daughters, Maria Hasan, Syeda Rabya Hasan and Ayesha Hasan for their continued moral support. This edition is an improved version benefiting from the inputs and feedback of all the well-wishers/readers. Mistakes and errors, if any, are mine.

Syed Hasan Javed

Syed Hasan Javed

سید حسن جاوید

About the Author

Syed Hasan Javed is an officer of the Foreign Service of Pakistan. He was born in 1955 and holds a B.A.(Honours) and M.A. degree in Economics from Karachi University. He joined the government service in 1979 after qualifying the Central Superior Services of Pakistan. He belongs to the 6th batch of the Common Training Program. He has served in different diplomatic assignments in Pakistani Embassies in Harare, Dushanbe and Brussels. He was also Pakistan's High Commissioner in Mauritius from 2003 to 2007.

He spent nearly a decade in the People's Republic of China, where he was first deputed to learn the Chinese language in September 1980 at the Beijing Institute of Languages. He completed advanced course in Chinese language before being posted in the Embassy of Pakistan in Beijing from 1982 to 1987 as third and second secretary respectively. He was deputed for the second time to work in the Pakistan Embassy in Beijing as the Deputy Head of Mission (Minister) from 2001 to 2003. Mr. Javed has travelled extensively in China. He has a deep interest and passion for Chinese language, culture, music, history, philosophy etc. He is currently posted as Pakistan's Commissioner in Singapore.

Introduction

The Chinese language's written script is based on the characters which have evolved from the ancient pictographs/symbols. The modern Chinese characters are the simplified version of the much complicated ancient forms (Gŭwẹ́nzì). The Chinese characters are known as (Hànzì). No body knows for sure, how many hànzì are there. The best estimate is between 15 to 20 thousands. In English language the number of alphabets is 26, in Arabic 32 and in Urdu 36, while in Chinese language there are no alphabets, but characters. A normal University graduate would know between five to eight thousand characters. Knowing five thousand characters would enable one to read a newspaper and any ordinary book. Some characters are words in themselves. For literary and technical disciplines, knowledge of ten thousand characters is required. The most scholary people claim to know 15,000 to 20,000 characters. Chinese written language is same in China and abroad. The spoken Chinese language, as compared to written text, is rather easier. The standard spoken mandarin follows four tones i.e. rising (/), (V) falling – rising (\) falling and neutral (-). Different regions in China speak their local dialects (dìfang yŭyán). For instance, the people of Shanghai speak Shanghai dialect, the people of Canton speak Cantonese. Similarly other regions have their own dialects. The mandarin (Putonghua) is Beijing based northern dialect. It is most commonly understood and used as medium of communication by all Chinese in China and abroad. Every Chinese loves deeply his language.

Speaking Chinese requires a constant practice of Pinyin tones by throat and tongue with nasal sounds (yŭdìao he yŭyīn). Only by repeated practice in a favourable environment (preferably with Chinese friends) or with CD cassettes can enable one to have a reasonable understanding and command of the language. It is difficult but achieveable. Studying of Chinese language requires great patience, hard work and perseverance. The fruit of this endeavour would be an awesome capacity to communicate with the one fourth of the world's population, win their hearts and minds and conduct business with the world's soon to be the largest economy and already the biggest exporter, who are also a trusted friend, neighbour, brother and strategic partner of Pakistan.

Pakistan China Friendship

China is our great neighbour and a brotherly country, which has stood by Pakistan in difficult times. China – Pakistan friendship is spread over several centuries. The former Chinese Premier Zhou Enlai had once stated! "China Pakistan friendship began with the advent of mankind". After the People's revolution in China in October, 1949, Pakistan recognised the new government in January 1950. A diplomatic mission was established on 21st May 1951. The close cooperation in political, economic, industrial, scientific, defence and cultural fields have given a unique place in the world to Pakistan – China friendship. Over the past six decades, China has made great achievements and exceeded its targets.

The Chinese economy had been growing at an average ten percent from 1980 - 2010. China has not only become the largest exporter but in a few years times, it is all set to be the world's largest economy. Its lead will continue by leaps and bounds. The rapid development and economic prosperity in China, is not only guarantee for peace and security in the world but also provides the world's largest market place. Pakistan is among the few countries, to share land border with China. There is tremendous good will between both countries at the popular and official level. Both countries have signed hundreds of Agreements including the Free Trade Agreement. Agreements between Pakistan and China span almost all sectors of human activity. There are enormous possibilities for promoting even closer cooperation in trade, investment and cultural fields in coming years.

The one billion four hundred million population of China and one hundred eighty million people of Pakistan in 2011 have to learn each other's language in order to promote long standing friendship. The exchanges between the two countries keep growing with the passage of time. With the prevalence of immense goodwill in the population of the two countries,the people of both countries are greatly fond of learning each other's language. The traders, officials and business people are particularly keen to speak in each other's language.

The writing of this book is to provide guidance to those people who wish to use basic conversation in Chinese for everyday use. For a structured course in the Chinese language, it is however necessary to get admission in a certified institute and learn the language formally through hard work, patience and practice.

History of Chinese Language

The history of the Chinese language is spread over several centuries. The centre of the Chinese civilization is the Yellow River (Huang He) which was also known as "Chinese sorrows", for its devastating floods in ancient times, as it changed its courses too often. The Chinese language provides the core identity to the Chinese civilization. The Chinese characters (visual representations of signs as against alphabets in other languages) has provided unity to Chinese identity and heritage. The Chinese language which is known as 'Mandarin' is also known as 'Putonghua (common speech) Zhongwen (language of China), Han yu (language of Han Chinese), Hua yu (Chinese people's language). The Chinese language is both an ancient and progressive language. The Chinese language is an evolutionary language in which every year, hundreds of words of other languages find their way in the closest meanings in the Chinese cultural context. In this assimilation process, the interpretor or the translator ensures common denominators of cultural interoperality, given China's own heritage in literature, social and cultural norms.

The beauty of Chinese language and civilization is that it has great capacity to benefit from other languages and civilizations and also benefit them. The standard Chinese i.e Mandarin follows four tones e.g rising, falling-rising, falling and neutral. The use of Romanised alphabets, also known as "Pinyin" helps the learning process. Without the right tones, it would be rather impossible to understand or be understood, while speaking Mandarin. It is important to remember that the Pinyin provides the closest approximation of the original sounds, and English alphabets do not correctly represent the meaning and sound of Chinese expressions.

Lesson-1

Chinese language sounds with examples- چینی زبان کی آواز مثال کے ساتھ , Hànyǔ yǔyīn, 汉语语音, Cheeni zaban ki awaz misaal kay saath

Pinyin	English	اُردو	چینی تلفظ	Roman Urdu
A Alābo	A Arab	اے عرب	آ آلابو	Arab
B Bājīsthăn	P Pakistan	ب پاکستان	پ پاچستھان	Be Pakistan
C Ca Càidān	Se Sa Menu	سے سا مِینو	سے صا صای تان	Se Sa Menu
Ch Chá	Th Tea	چ چائے	ٹِھ ٹِھا آ	Che Chai
D Dà	T Big	د بڑا	ت تا	Dal Barra
G Gănxiè	K To Thank	گ شکریہ کرنا	ک کان شِیے	Gaf Shukrya Karna
H Hăo	H Good	ح اچھا	خ خاو	Hey Achcha
J Jī	Ch Chicken	ج مُرغی	چ چِی	Jeem Murghi
K Kāishĭ	K To begin	ک شُروع کرنا	کَھ کھاءی شِی	Kaf Shuru Karna
P Páshān	P Climb Hill	پ پہاڑ پر چڑھنا	پھ پھَا شآن	Pe Pahar par Charhna

Pinyin	English	اُردو	چینی تلفظ	Roman Urdu
Qi Qī	Chi Seven	کی سات	چھِی چھِی	Ki Saat
R Rè Le	R Hungry	رے بھوک لگنا	غے غا-لہ	Re Bhook Lagna
S Sān	S Three	س تین	سے سان	Seen Teen
Sh Shàngdi	Xi God	ش خُدا تعالٰی	شِی شنگ تی	Sheen Khuda Taala
T Tā	Th He/She	ت وہ	تھِ تھا	Te Woh
Xi Xī	Shi West	ژِی مغرب	شِی شِی	Shi Maghrib
Yi Yī	I One	یِ ایک	اِی اِی	Ye Eik
Yu Yŭ	Yu Rain	یواِی یواِی	اِیوی اِیوی	Yuyi Yuyi
Z Zàijiàn	Z See you again	ذ پھر ملیں گے	ذِ ذآی چیان	Ze Phir milinge
Zh Zhè (ge)	Ch This (one)	چ [ژ] یہ [والا]	چے / ژے چیگا	Che Yeh (wala)

Lesson-2

Counting – گنتی , Shùzì, 数字, Geenti

Chinese	Pinyin	English	اُردو	چینی تلفظ	Roman Urdu
零	Líng	Zero	صفر	لِینگ	Sifar
一	Yī	One	ایک	اِی (یو)	Ek
二	Èr	Two	دو	اَر	Do
三	Sān	Three	تین	سَن	Teen
四	Sì	Four	چار	سِی	Char
五	Wǔ	Five	پانچ	اُوو	Paanch
六	Liù	Six	چھ	لِیو	Chay
七	Qī	Seven	سات	چھی	Saat
八	Bā	Eight	آٹھ	پَا	Aath
九	Jiǔ	Nine	نو	چِیو	No
十	Shí	Ten	دس	شِ	Das
十一	Shíyī	Eleven	گیارہ	شِ ای	Giyara
十九	Shíjiǔ	Nineteen	اُنیس	شِ چِیو	Unees
二十	Èrshí	Twenty	بیس	اَرِ ش	Bees
九十	Jiǔshí	Ninety	نوے	چیوِ ش	Naawe
一百	Yī bǎi	One hun-dred	ایک سو	اِی پائے	Ek So
一千	Yīqiān	One thou-sand	ایک ہزار	اِی چھیان	Ek Hazar
一万	Yī wàn	Ten thou-sand	دس ہزار	اِی وآن	Das Hazar
十亿	Shí yì	One billion	ایک ارب	شِ اِی	Ek Arab

Lesson-3

Chinese grammar - چینی گرامر, Hànyǔ yǔfǎ, 汉语语法, Cheeni grammar

Chinese	Pinyin	English	اُردو	چینی تلفظ	Roman Urdu
名词	Míngcí	Noun	اِسم	مینگسہ	Ism
代词	Dàicí	Pronoun	ضمیر	طائے سی	Zameer
动词	DòngCí	Verb	فعل	دونگسہ	Fel
形容词	XíngRóngCí	Adjective	صفت	شی رونگسہ	Sifat
副词	FùCí	Adverb	مفعول	فو سی	Mafool
数词	Shù Cí	Numeral	اعداد	شُو سی	Edad
量词	LiàngCí	Measure words	میزانِ الفاظ	لیانگسی	Meezan Alfaz
介词	JièCí	Preposition	حُرف جار	چیے سی	Hurf Rabt
连词	LianCí	Conjunc-tion	حُرف ربط	لیا نسی	Hurf Rabt
助词	ZhùCí	Particle	حُرف سابقہ	جُو سی	Hurf Sabqa
生词	ShēngCí	Word	لفظ	شنگسی	Lafz

Lesson-4

Animals and Birds- حیوانات اور پرندے, Dòngwù/niǎo er, 动物／鸟, Hawanat aur Parande

Chinese	Pinyin	English	اُردو	چینی تلفظ	Roman Urdu
龙	Lóng	Dragon	اژدھا	لونگ	Azdaha
大象	Dà xiàng	Elephant	ہاتھی	تا شیانگ	Hathi
老虎	Lǎohǔ	Tiger	چیتا	لاؤخو	Cheeta
狮子	Shīzi	Lion	ببر شیر	شی زہ	Babar Sher
蛇	Shé	Snake	سانپ	شی	Saanp
猴子	Hóuzi	Monkey	بندر	خو زہ	Bandar
猫	Māo	Cat	بلّی	ما آؤ	Billi
熊猫	Xióngmāo	Panda	پینڈا	شیونگ مو	Panda
狼	Láng	Wolf	بھیڑیا	لانگ	Bheriya
狗	Gǒu	Dog	کُتا	گُوو	Kutta
猪	Zhū	Pig	سوّر	جُو	Suuar
羊	Yáng	Sheep	بھیڑ	یانگ	Bher
山羊	Shānyáng	Goat	بکری	شان یانگ	Bakri
鸡	Jī	Chicken	مرغی	چی	Murghi
青蛙	Qīngwā	Frog	مینڈک	چھنگ وا	Mendak
鱼	Yú	Fish	مچھلی	اِیوی	Machli
虾	Xiā	Prawn	جھینگا	ہائی شیا	Jheenga
马	Mǎ	Horse	گھوڑا	ما	Ghora
熊	Xióng	Bear	ریچھ	شیونگ	Reech
驴	Lǘ	Donkey	گدھا	لو	Gadha
鸟	Niǎo	Bird	چڑیا	نِیاؤ	Cheerya
牛	Niú	Cow	گائے	نیو	Gaay

Lesson-5

Countries - ممالک کے نام, Guójiā, 国家, Mumalik ke Nam

Chinese	Pinyin	English	اُردو	چینی تلفظ	Roman Urdu
国家	Guójiā	Country	ملک	کوچیا	Mulk
世界	Shìjiè	World	دُنیا	شی چیے	Dunya
亚洲	Yàzhōu	Asia	ایشیاء	یاچو	Asia
巴基斯坦	Bājīsītǎn	Pakistan	پاکستان	پاچستھان	Pakistan
中国	Zhōngguó	China	چین	چونگوآ	Chin
美国	Měiguó	USA	امریکہ	میگوآ	Amerika
英国	Yīngguó	UK	اِنگلستان	اِینگوآ	Englistan
沙特阿拉伯	Shātè ālābó	Saudi Arabia	سعودی عرب	شاتھ آلابو	Saudi Arabia
阿联酋	Āliánqiú	UAE	عرب امارات	آلیان	Arab Ema-rat
伊朗	Yīlǎng	Iran	ایران	اِی لانگ	Iran
印度	Yìndù	India	ہندوستان	اِین دُو	Hindustan
阿富汗	Āfùhàn	Afghani-stan	افغانستان	آفو خان	Afghani-stan
印尼	Yìnní	Indonesia	انڈونیشیا	اِینی	Indonesia

Chinese	Pinyin	English	اُردو	چینی تلفظ	Roman Urdu
澳大利亚	Àodàlìyǎ	Australia	آسٹریلیا	اوڈالیا	Australia
土耳其	Tǔ'ěrqí	Turkey	ترکی	تُھوآرچھی	Turkey
埃及	Āijí	Egypt	مصر	آئیچی	Misr
孟加拉国	Mèng-jiālāguó	Bangladesh	بنگلہ دیش	مِن چیلاکوآ	Bangladesh
日本	Rìběn	Japan	جاپان	ری بین	Japan
巴西	Bāxī	Brazil	برازیل	پاشی	Brazil
南非	Nánfēi	South Africa	جنوبی افریقہ	نان ـفے	Janubi Africa
加拿大	Jiānádà	Canada	کینیڈا	چیاناڈا	Canada
法国	Fàguó	France	فرانس	فاگوآ	France
德国	Déguó	Germany	جرمنی	دَگوآ	Germany
瑞士	Ruìshì	Switzer-land	سوءزلینڈ	ِر شِر	Switzer-land

Lesson-6

Names of languages–Yǔyán, زبانوں کے نام 语言Zabanon ke Nam

Chinese	Pinyin	English	اُردو	چینی تلفظ	Roman Urdu
汉语	Hànyǔ	Chinese	چینی	خان ایوی	Cheeni
英语	Yīngyǔ	English	انگریزی	اِینگ یوئی	Engrezi
乌尔都语	Wū ěr dū yǔ	Urdu	اردو	اُوآردویوی	Urdu
阿拉伯语	Ālābó yǔ	Arabic	عربی	آلابوویوی	Arbi
波斯语	Bōsī yǔ	Persian	فارسی	پوسووین	Farsi
印地语	Yìn dì yǔ	Hindi	ہندی	اِندوِیوی	Hindi
俄语	É yǔ	Russian	روسی	عَاییو	Rusi
德语	Déyǔ	German	جرمن	داویں	German
西班牙语	Xībānyá yǔ	Spanish	ہسپانوی	شی بانیاوی	Hispanwi
日语	Rì yǔ	Japanese	جاپانی	رویوی	Japani
法语	Fǎyǔ	French	فرانسیسی	فا اِیوی	Fransisi

Lesson-7

Continents, Oceans- Mountains - برآعظم ، بحر ، پہاڑ
Dàzhōu, hǎi, shān,
大洲，海，山 Bare-Azam,Bahr,Pahar

Chinese	Pinyin	English	اُردو	چینی تلفظ	Roman Urdu
世界	Shìjiè	World	دنیا	شی چے	Dunya
亚洲	Yàzhōu	Asia	ایشیا	یا آچو	Asia
非洲	Fēizhōu	Africa	افریقہ	فے چو	Afrika
欧洲	Ōuzhōu	Europe	یورپ	اوچو	Europe
美国	Měiguó	America	امریکہ	مے چو	Amerika
太平洋	Tàipíngyáng	Pacific Ocean	بحرہ الکاہل	تھائی پنگ یانگ	Bahr-e-Kahil
印度洋	Yìndùyáng	Indian Ocean	بحرہ ہند	اِندو یانگ	Bahr-e-Hind
阿拉伯海	Ālābó hǎi	Arabian Sea	بحرہ عرب	آلا بو ہائے	Bahr-e-Arab
波斯湾	Bōsī wān	Persian Gulf	خلیج فارس	پوسو و آن ہائے	Khaleej-Faras
喜马拉雅山	Xǐmǎlāyǎ shān	Himala-yas	ہمالیہ	شِمالیہ شان	Himalaya
喀喇昆仑	Kā lǎ kūnlún	Karako-rum	قراہ قرم	کالا کولون	Karakorum
昆仑	Kūnlún	Kunlun	کُن لُن	کُن لُن	Kunlun
天山	Tiānshān	Heaven-lyMoun-tains	کوہ بہشتی	تھیان شان	Koh-i-Tian

Lesson-8

Religions and Culture - مذاہب اور ثقافت, Zōngjiào/wén-huà，宗教／文化 Mazahib aur Saqafat

Chinese	Pinyin	English	اُردو	چینی تلفظ	Roman Urdu
伊斯兰教	Yīsīlán jiào	Islam	اسلام	اِسلان چِیاؤ	Islam
基督教	Jīdūjiào	Christianity	عیسائیت	چِیتُو چِیاؤ	Isayat
佛教	Fójiào	Buddhism	بُدھ مت	فُو چِیاؤ	Budhmat
犹太教	Yóutàijiào	Judaism	یہودیت	یُو آن چِیاؤ	Yehudiyat
喇嘛教	Lǎmajiào	Lamaism	لامازم	لاما چِیاؤ	Lamaism
儒教	Rújiào	Confucian-ism	کنفیوشیزم	کھونگفوچِیاؤ	Confucian-ism
道教	Dàojiào	Taoism	تاؤاِزم	تاؤ چِیاؤ	Taoism
真主	Zhēnzhǔ	Allah	اللہ	ڑین چُو	Allah
穆罕默德	Mù hǎn mò dé	Muham-mad	محمد ﷺ	مُحمّد ﷺ	Muham-mad-(p.b.u.h)
先知	Xiānzhī	Prophet	پیغمبر	شیان ڑ	Peghamber
清真	Qīngzhēn	Pure	حلال	چھینگ ڑین	Halal
清真寺	Qīngzhēnsì	Mosque	مسجد	چھینگ ڑینسی	Masjid
祈祷	Qídǎo	Prayer	نماز	چھی تاؤ	Nemaz
穆斯林	Mùsīlín	Muslim	مسلمان	مو سلین	Musalman
禁食	Jìn shí	Fasting	روزہ	چِن شِر	Roza

Chinese	Pinyin	English	اُردو	چینی تلفظ	Roman Urdu
开斋节	Kāizhāi jié	Eid-ul-Fitr	عیدالفطر	کھائی ژاے چی ے	Eid-ul-Fitr
圣诞节	Shèngdàn jié	Christmas	کرسمس	شنگٹھان چی ے	Christmas
春节	Chūnjié	Spring Festival Lunar New Year	موسم بہاراں	ٹھون چی ے	Mau-sim-e-Baha-ran
国庆节	Guóqìng jié	National Day Fes-tival	قومی دن تہوار	کوچھنگ چی ے	Qau-mi-Din,Te-hwar

Lesson-9

Currency and Time - پیسہ اور وقت , Qián/shíjiān， 钱／时间Paisa aur Waqt

Chinese	Pinyin	English	اُردو	چینی تلفظ	Roman Urdu
人民币	Rénmínbì	People's currency	یو آن	رینمین بی	Yuan
元（块）	Yuán (Kuài)	Yuan	یو آن	یو آن	Yuan
角/ 毛	Jiǎo / Máo	One Tenth of a Dollar / Ten cents	ماؤ	چیاؤ (ماؤ)	Mao
分	Fēn	Cent	سینٹ	فِین	Cent
一块＝十角/十分＝一毛	Yīkuài = shí Jiǎo /shí Fēn = yī máo	1 Yuan = One Tenth of a Yuan / ten cents	ایک یو آن برابر ۔ دس ماو	ای کھوائی ۔ شی ماو	Ek Yuan bra-bar das Mao.
一毛/一角＝十分	Yī máo/ Yī Jiǎo = shí fēn	One Tenth of a Yuan = 10 Cents	یو آن کا دسواں حصہ	اِی ماؤ ۔ شی فین	Ek Mao bra-bar das Fen
卢比	Lúbǐ	Rupees	روپیہ	لُوبی	Rupiah
美元	Měiyuán	US Dollar	امریکی ڈالر	مے یو آن	Amriki Dollar
几点了？	Jǐ diǎnle?	What time is it?	کیا وقت ہے؟	چی تیان لہ	Kiya waqt hai?
现在十二点了	Xiànzài shí'èr diǎnle	It is 12 o'clock	ابھی بارہ بجے ہیں	شیان ذاے شر ارتیان لہ	Abhi barah baje hain.

Chinese	Pinyin	English	اُردو	چینی تلفظ	Roman Urdu
一天有二十四个小时	Yītiān yǒu èrshísì gè xiǎoshí	One day has 24 twenty four hours	ایک دن میں چوبیس گھنٹے ہوتے ہیں	اِی تھیان یو ار شی سیگا شیاو شر۔	Ek din mein chobis ghante hote hain.
早上	Zǎoshang	Morning	صبح	زوشینگ	Subah
中午	Zhōngwǔ	Noon	دوپہر	چُونگ اُو	Dopahar
下午	Xiàwǔ	Afternoon	سپہر	شِیا اُو	Sepahar
晚上	Wǎnshàng	Evening	شام	وآن شنگ	Shaam
夜间	Yèjiān	Night	رات	یے چیان	Raat
白天	Báitiān	Day	دن	پائے تھیان	Din
早上好	Zǎoshang hǎo	Good Morning	صبح البخیر	زاؤشینگ خاؤ	Sub-ah-al-Khair
晚上好	Wǎnshàng hǎo	Good Evening	شام بخیر	وآن شنگ خاؤ	Shaam-Bakhair

Lesson-10

Direction - سمت , Fāngxiàng, 方向 Simt

Chinese	Pinyin	English	اُردو	چینی تلفظ	Roman Urdu
方向	Fāngxiàng	Direction	سمت	فنگ شیانگ	Seemt
东	Dōng	East	مشرق	تونگ	Mashriq
西	Xī	West	مغرب	شی	Maghrib
南	Nán	South	جنوب	نان	Janub
北	Běi	North	شمال	پے	Shumal
东方	Dōng (fāng)	Eastern	مشرقی	تونگ فانگ	Mashriqi
西方	Xī (fāng)	Western	مغربی	شی فانگ	Maghribi
南方	Nán (fāng)	Southern	جنوبی	نان فانگ	Janubi
北方	Běi (fāng)	Northern	شمالی	پے فانگ	Shumali
上	Shàng	Up	اوپر	شنگ	Upar
下	Xià	Down	نیچے	شیا	Neeche
里	Lǐ	In	اندر	لی	Under
外	Wài	Outside	باہر	وائے	Bahar

Chinese	Pinyin	English	اُردو	چینی تلفظ	Roman Urdu
前	Qián	Front	سامنے	چھیان	Samne
后	Hòu	Back	پیچھے	خو	Peeche
旁	Páng	Side	ساتھ	پھانگ	Sath
中	Zhōng	Middle	درمیان	چُونگ	Darmian

Add 'bian' to each of the above to get the desired meaning For example:

پیان لگائیں۔ مثال کے طور پر

Shàngbiān – Upside --Upar

شنگ پیان
بالائی / اوپر

Xià biān – Downside--Neeche

شیاپیان -
زیریں / نیچے

Wàibiān – Outside --Bahar

وائے پیان
خارجی / باہر

Lesson-11

Measurements - ناپ تول, Liàngcí , 量词 Naap Toal

Chinese	Pinyin	English	اُردو	چینی تلفظ	Roman Urdu
公斤	Gōngjīn	Kilogram	کیلو	کونگ چِن	Kilo
半公斤	Bàn gōng-jīn	Half kilo	آدھا کیلو	پَن کونگ چِن	Adh kilo
一斤	Yī jīn	Half kilo	آدھا کیلو	اِی چِن	Adh kilo
一英磅	Yī yīngbàng	One En-glishpound	ایک انگریزی پاؤنڈ	اِی اینگ پانگ	Ek pond
一尺	Yī chǐ	One foot	ایک فٹ	اِی ٹھی	Ek foot
一米	Yī mǐ	One meter	ایک میٹر	اِی مِی	Ek meter
一公里	Yī gōnglǐ	One kilo-meter	ایک کلو میٹر	اِی کونگ لی	Ek kilome-ter
半公里	Bàn gōnglǐ	Half kilo-meter	نصف کلو میٹر	پان کونگ	Adh kilo-meter
长	Cháng	Long	لمبا	ٹھانگ	Lamba
宽	Kuān	Wide	چوڑائی	کھوآن	Chora
深	Shēn	Depth	گہرائی	شِین	Gahra
胖	Pàng	Fat	موٹائی	پھانگ	Mota
高	Gāo	High	اونچا	کاؤ	Uncha
小	Xiǎo	Small	چھوٹا	شیاؤ	Chota

Chinese	Pinyin	English	اُردو	چینی تلفظ	Roman Urdu
大	Dà	Big	بڑا	تا	Bara
个子	Gèzi	Height	قد	کاذا	Qad
几个	Jǐ gè	How many?	کتنا	چیگہ	Kitna
几点了	Jǐ diǎnle	What time is the?	کیا وقت ہے؟	چی تیان لہ	Kiya Waq -t Hai
一点了	Yīdiǎnle	It's one o'clock	ایک بجا ہے۔	اِی تیان لہ	Ek Baja Hai
一天	Yītiān	One day	ایک دن	اِی تھیان	Ek din

Lesson-12

Address - خطاب , Chēnghu, 称呼Khetab

Chinese	Pinyin	English	اردو	چینی تلفظ	Roman Urdu
我	Wǒ	I	میں	وُو	Main
我们	Wǒmen	We	ہم لوگ	وُومین	Hum log
你	Nǐ	You	تُم	نِی	Tum
你们	Nǐmen	You (plural)	تُم لوگ	نِی مین	Tum log
他/她	Tā/tā	He/she	وہ	تھا	Woh
他们	Tāmen	They	وہ لوگ	تھا مین	Who log
他的	Tā de	His/her	اس کا /اس کی	تھا دا	Us/Us ka
他们的	Tāmen de	Their/ theirs	اُن لوگوں کا	تھا مین دا	Un ka
你的	Nǐ de	Your/yours	تمہارا/تمہاری	نِی دا	Tumha-ra/ ri

Chinese	Pinyin	English	اردو	چینی تلفظ	Roman Urdu
你们的	Nǐmen de	Your/yours (plural)	تُم لوگوں کا	نِی مین دا	Tum Logon ka
我的	Wǒ de	Mine	میرا/میری	وُدا	Mera/ri
我们/我们的	Wǒmen/ wǒmen de	Our/ours	ہمارا / ہماری	وُومین دا	Hamara/ Hamari
先生	Xiānshēng	Mr.	جناب / صاحب	شیان شنگ	Janab
夫人	Fūrén	Madam	بیگم	فُورین	Begum
小姐	Xiǎojiě	Miss	محترمہ	شیاؤ چیئے	Mohtarma
同志	Tóngzhì	Comrade	ساتھی	ٹھونگ ٹر	Saathi
教师	Lǎo	Teacher	اُستاد	لاو شِر	Ustad
朋友	Péngyǒu	Friend	دوست	پھانگ یو	Dost
师父	Shīfu	Technician	ہُنر مند	شِر فو	Hunar -mand
小孩	Xiǎohái	Child	بچہ	شیاوہر	Bacha

Lesson-13

Family relationships- خاندانی رشتے ناطے , Jiātíng guānxì ，家庭关系Khandani Rishtay Naatay

Chinese	Pinyin	English	اُردو	چینی تلفظ	Roman Urdu
家	Jiā	Family	خاندان	چِیا	Khandan
妈妈	Māmā	Mother	ماں	مَاما	Ma
母亲	Mŭqīn	Mother	والدہ	مُوچھن	Walida
爸爸	Bà ba	Father	باپ	پاپا	Baap
父亲	Fùqīn	Dad	والد	فُوچھن	Walid
大爷	Dàyé	Eldest uncle	بڑے ابّا	تائے	Bare Abba/ Taye
姐姐	Jiejie	Elder sister	بڑی بہن	چِیئے چِیئے	Bari Bahan
妹妹	Mèimei	Younger sister	چھوٹی بہن	مِے مِے	Choti Ba-han
哥哥	Gēgē	Elder brother	بڑا بھائی	کہ گا	Bara Bhai
弟弟	Dìdì	Younger brother	چھوٹا بھائی	دِی دِی	Chota Bhai
祖父	Zŭfù	Grand dad	دادا/نانا	ذُوفو	Dada/Nana

Chinese	Pinyin	English	اُردو	چینی تلفظ	Roman Urdu
祖母	Zǔmǔ	Grandma	دادی/نانی	زُو مُو	Dadi/Nani
叔叔	Shūshu	Uncle	چچا	شُو شُو	Chacha
舅舅	Jiùjiu	Maternal uncle	ماموں	چیو چِیو	Mamun
姨妈	Āyí	Aunt	چچی۔ ممانی۔ پھوپھی	آئی	Chachi/ Mumani/ Phuphi
嫂子	Sǎozi	Brother's wife	بھابھی	ساوزا	Bhabi
姑娘	Gūniang	Girl	لڑکی	کونیانگ	Larki
丈夫	Zhàngfū	Husband	شوہر	چانگ فُو	Shauhar
爱人	Àirén	Spouse	بیوی/شوہر	آئی رین	Biwee/ Shauhar
儿子	Érzi	Son	بیٹا	اَرزہ	Beta
女儿	Nǚ'ér	Daughter	بیٹی	نیو آر	Betee
男人	Nánrén	Man	مرد	نان رین	Mard
女人	Nǚrén	Woman	عورت	نیو رین	Aurat

Lesson-14

Attending a Conference - کانفرنس میں شرکت Cānjiā huì，参加会Kanference me shirkat

Chinese	Pinyin	English	اُردو	چینی تلفظ	Roman Urdu
代表团	Dàibiǎo tuán	Delegation	وفد	تائی پیاؤ تھوآن	Wafd
国际	Guójì	Interna-tional	بین لاقوامی	کواوجی	Bain-ul-Aqwami
团长	Tuán zhǎng	Head of delegation	وفد کا سربراہ	تھُوآن ترانگ	Wafd ka Sarbarah
庆祝	Qìngzhù	To cele-brate	جشن منانا	چھنگ ٹو	Jashn Ma-nana
代表	Dàibiǎo	Delegate	نمائندہ	تائی پیاو	Numainda
主席台	Zhǔxí tái	Rostrum	ممبر	جُو شی تائے	Rostrum
观众	Guānzhòng	Audience	حاضرین	کوآن چونگ	Nazirin
集合	Jíhé	To assem-ble	جمع کرنا	چِی خا	Jama Karna
讲话	Jiǎnghuà	Make a speech	تقریر کرنا	چِیانگ خوآ	Taqrir Karna

Chinese	Pinyin	English	اُردو	چینی تلفظ	Roman Urdu
最后	Zuìhòu	Finally	آخر میں	ژُوئی ہو	Akhir Me
参加	Cānjiā	Participate	حصہ لینا	صان چیا	Hissa Lena
晚宴/晚夕会	Wǎnhuì	Evening reception	عشائیہ	وآن خوئی	Eshaa-ya
展览会	Zhǎnlǎn huì	Exhibition	میلہ	چان لان خوئی	Mela
讨论会	Tǎolùn huì	Seminar	سیمینار	تھاولن خوئی	Seminar
招待会	Zhāodài huì	Reception	استقبالیہ	چاؤتاءِخوئی	Istaqbalia

Lesson-15

Days – Week – Months دن۔ ہفتہ ۔ مہینے - Tiān, lĭbài, yuè，天, 礼拜, 月 Din,Hafte,Maheenay

Chinese	Days	English	اُردو	چینی تلفظ	Roman Urdu
星期日	Xīngqírì	Sunday	اتوار	شِینگ چھی نی	Etwar
星期一	Xīngqí yī	Monday	پیر	شِینگ چھی اِی	Peer
星期二	Xīngqí èr	Tuesday	منگل	شِینگ چھی ار	Mangal
星期三	Xīngqí sān	Wednes-day	بُدھ	شینگ چھی سان	Budh
星期四	Xīngqí sì	Thursday	جمعرات	شنگ چھی سِی	Jumrat
星期五	Xīngqí wŭ	Friday	جمعہ	شنگ چھی اُو	Jumma
星期六	Xīngqí liù	Saturday	ہفتہ	شِنگ چھی لِیو	Hafta
今天	Jīntiān	Today	آج	چِن تھیان	Aaj
明天	Míngtiān	Tomorrow	کل	مِنگ تھیان	Kal
昨天	Zuótiān	Yesterday	گذشتہ کل	زو تھیان	Guzista Kal
前天	Qiántiān	Day before yesterday	گزری پرسوں	چھیان تھیان	Kuzri Par-sun
后天	Hòutiān	Day after tomorrow	آنے والی پرسوں	خو تھیان	Anay Wali Parsun
月	Yuè	Month	مہینہ	یُو وے	Mahina
月亮	Yuèliàng	Moon	چاند	یو وے لیانگ	Chand
太阳	Tàiyáng	Sun	سورج	تھائی یانگ	Suraj
早上	Zăoshang	Morning	صبح	ذاؤ شینگ	Subah
晚上	Wănshàng	Evening	شام	وآن شنگ	Shaam

Lesson-16

Seasons and Months – موسم اور مہینے , Jì/yuè，季／月 Mausam aur Maheenay

Chinese	Pinyin	English	اُردو	چینی تلفظ	Roman Urdu
今年	Jīnnián	Current year	موجودہ سال	چِین نیان	Maujuda Sal
明年	Míngnián	Next year	اگلا سال	مِینگ نیان	Agla Sal
去年	Qùnián	Last year	گزشتہ سال	چھوئی نیان	Guzista Sal
夏季	Xiàjì	Summer	گرمی	شیا چِھی	Garmi
秋天	Qiūtiān	Autumn	خزاں	چھیو تھیان	Khezan
冬天	Dōngtiān	Winter	سردی	تونگ تھیان	Sardi
春天	Chūntiān	Spring	بہار	ٹھوئن تھیان	Bahar
一月	Yī yuè	January	جنوری	اِی یُووے	January
二月	Èr yuè	February	فروری	اَر یُووے	February
三月	Sān yuè	March	مارچ	سان یُووے	March
四月	Sì yuè	April	اپریل	سی یُووے	April
五月	Wǔ yuè	May	مئی	اُوو یُووے	May
六月	Liù yuè	June	جون	لِیو یُووے	June
七月	Qī yuè	July	جولائی	چِھی یُووے	July
八月	Bā yuè	August	اگست	پَاآیُووے	August

Chinese	Pinyin	English	اُردو	چینی تلفظ	Roman Urdu
九月	Jiŭ yuè	September	ستمبر	چیو یُووے	September
十月	Shíyuè	October	اکتوبر	شی یُووے	October
十一月	Shíyī yuè	November	نومبر	شی اِی یُووے	November
十二月	Shí'èr yuè	December	دسمبر	شی ار یُووے	December
一年	Yī nián	One year	ایک سال	اِی نیان	Ek Sal
十年	Shí nián	Ten years	دس سال	شی نیان	Das Sal
世紀	Shìjì	Century	صد سال	شی جی	Sad Sal
萬歲	Wànsuì	Ten thousand years	دس ہزار سال	وآن سُوئی	Das Hazar

Lesson-17

Body and Health – جسم اور صحت , Shēn/shēntǐ，身／身体 Jism Aur Sehat

Chinese	Pinyin	English	اردو	چینی تلفظ	Roman Urdu
健康	Jiànkāng	Healthy	صحت مند	چیان کھانگ	Sehat mund
身体	Shēntǐ	Health	صحت	شینتھی	Sehat
身	Shēn	Body	جسم	شین	Jism
头	Tóu	Head	سر	تھوو	Sar
嘴	Zuǐ	Mouth	مُنہ	ذُوئی	Munh
手	Shǒu	Hand	ہاتھ	شو	Hath
眼睛	Yǎnjīng	Eye	آنکھ	یان چنگ	Ankh
鼻子	Bízi	Nose	ناک	پِی ذہ	Nak
牙	Yá	Teeth	دانت	یا	Dan't
呼吸	Hūxī	To breathe	سانس لینا	خو شی	Sans Lena
脚	Jiǎo	Feet	پیر	چیاؤ	Pa'er
病	Bìng le	Fall sick	بیمار ہونا	پینگ لہ	Bimar Hona
肚子	Dùzi	Stomach	پیٹ	تُو ذہ	Pe't
血	Xuè	Blood	خون	شِی ے	Khoon

Chinese	Pinyin	English	اُردو	چینی تلفظ	Roman Urdu
血压	Xiěyā	Blood pressure	بلڈ پریشر	شیے یا	Blood pressure
嗓子	Sǎngzi	Throat	گلہ / آواز	سانگزہ	Galaa
咳嗽	Késou	To cough	کھانسی	کھہ ساؤ	Khan'see
头疼	Tóuténg	Headache	سر درد	تھوتھنگ	Sar Dard
肚子疼	Dùzi téng	Stomach ache	پیٹ کا درد	ٹوزہ تھنگ	Pe't ka dard
感冒	Gǎnmào	Flu (cold)	نزلہ ذکام	کان ماؤ	Nazla Zukam
发烧	Fāshāo	Fever	بخار	فاشاؤ	Bukhar
扁桃体	Biǎntáotǐ	Tonsil	تونسل	بیان تھاؤتھی	Tonsil
糖尿病	Táng-niàobìng	Diabetic	ذیابطیس	تھانگ لیاؤ پنگ	Ziab-tees
心脏病	Xīnzàng bìng	Heart/cardiac	دل دھڑکن	شن ذانگ پنگ	Dil dharkan
医生	Yīshēng	Doctor	ڈاکٹر	اِی شینگ	Daktor
护士	Hùshì	Nurse	نرس	خوشی	Nurse
中医/中药	Zhōng yīliáo	Chinese medicine	چینی دوا	چونگ ایلیاؤ	Cheeni Dawa
医院	Yīyuàn	Hospital	ہسپتال	اِی یوان	Haspatal

Lesson-18

Education - تعلیم , Jiàoyù ，教育 Ta'leem

Chinese	Pinyin	English	اُردو	چینی تلفظ	Roman Urdu
教育	Jiàoyù	Education	تعلیم	چیاؤ ایوی	Ta'leem
工程	Gōngchéng	Engineer-ing	انجنیرنگ	کونگ ٹھنگ شُوے	Engineer-ing
医学	Yīxué	Medical studies	میڈیکل	اِی شوے	Medical
生意	Shēngyì	Business studies	بزنس	شنگ اِی شُوے	Business
经济学	Jīngjì xué	Econom-ics	علم اقتصاد	چینگ چی شُوے	Ilm-e-Ikte-sad
天文学	Tiānkōng xué	Astronau-tics	علم فلکیات	تھیان کھونگ شُوے	Ilm-e Falkiat
学文学	Wényì xué	Literature	ادبیات	وینی شُوے	Adab'yiat
历史学	Lìshǐ xué	History	تاریخ	لِی شِی شوے	Tareekh
地理学	Dìlǐ xué	Geology	ارضیات	تی لی شُوے	Arziat
化学	Huàxué	Chemical studies	علم کیمیا	خوآشُوے	Ilm-e-Ke-mikal
站略学	Zhànlì xué	Strategic studies	علم اسٹریٹیجی	تران لی شُوے	Ilm-e-Is-trategy
军事学	Jūnshì xué	Military studies	فوجی تعلیم	چوءن شی شُوے	Fauji Taleem
文学研究	Wénhuà xué	Cultural studies	علم فرہنگ	وِین خو شُوے	Ilm-e-Far-hang
地震学	Dìzhèn xué	Seismol-ogy	علم ذلزلہ	تِی ٹرنگ شُوے	Ilm-e-Zal-zala

Chinese	Pinyin	English	اردو	چینی تلفظ	Roman Urdu
老师	Lǎoshī	Teacher	اُستاد	لاؤ شی	Ustad
教师	Jiàoshī	Professor	پروفیسر	چیاؤ شی	Professor
毕业	Bìyè	Graduate	گریجویٹ	پی یے	Graduate
硕士	Shuòshì	Master degree	ایم اے	سُوو شی	M.A
博士	Bóshì	PhD	ڈاکٹر	پوشی	Doctor
学生	Xuéshēng	Student	طالب علم	شُوے شنگ	Talib-Ilm
研究	Yánjiū	Research	تحقیق	یان چیو	Tahqeeq
大学	Dàxué	University	جامعہ	تا شُوے	Jame'a
高中学校	Gāo zhōngxué xiào	College	کالج	کاؤ چنگ شوے شیاؤ	College
学校	Xuéxiào	School	اسکول	شُوے شیاؤ	School

Lesson-19

Supermarket – سُپر مارکیٹ , Shìchǎng，市场 Supermarket

Chinese	Pinyin	English	اُردو	چینی تلفظ	Roman Urdu
鸡	Jī	Chicken	مُرغی	چِی	Murghi
肉	Ròu	Meat	گوشت	رو	Gosht
牛肉	Niú Ròu	Beef	گائے کا گوشت	نیو رو	Gai ka Gosht
羊肉	Yáng Ròu	Mutton	بھیڑ کا گوشت	یانگ رو	Bher ka Gosht
山羊肉	Shānyáng Ròu	Goat	بکرے کا گوشت	شان یانگ رو	Bakre ka Gosht
鸡蛋	Jīdàn	Eggs	انڈے	چی دان	An'de
水	Shuǐ	Water	پانی	شوئی	Pa'nee
汽水	Qìshuǐ	Soft drink	سوفٹ ڈرنک	چھی شوئی	Soft drink
果汁	Guǒzhī	Fruit juice	پھل کا رس	گُووڈھر	Phal ka rus
苹果	Píngguǒ	Apple	سیب	پھنگ گوآ	Se'b
芒果	Mángguǒ	Mango	آم	مَان گوآ	A'am
西瓜	Xīguā	Water melon	تربوز	شی گوآ	Tarbuz
梨子	Lízi	Pear	ناشپاتی	لیزہ	Nashpati
橙子	Chéngzi	Orange	نارنجی	چُوئی ذہ	Naranji

Chinese	Pinyin	English	اُردو	چینی تلفظ	Roman Urdu
葡萄	Pútáo	Grapes	انگور	پھوتھاؤ	Angoor
香蕉	Xiāngjiāo	Banana	کیلا	شیانگ چیاؤ	Ke'la
桃子	Táozi	Peach	آڑو	تھاؤزہ	A'ru
辣椒	Làjiāo	Chilli	ہری مرچ	لاچیاؤ	Hari Mirch
土豆	Tǔdòu	Potato	آلو	تھُوتھاؤ	A'loo
葱头	Cōngtóu	Onion	پیاز	سُنگ تھاؤ	Pi'yaz
西红柿	Xīhóngshì	Tomato	ٹماٹر	شی خونگ سی	Tama'tar
黄瓜	Huángguā	Cucumber	کھیرا	خوانگ گوا	Kheera
白菜	Báicài	Chinese cabbage	چینی سلاد	پائی صائی	Cheeni Salad
蔬菜	Shūcài	Vegetable	سبزیاں	شوسائی	Sab'zian
牛奶	Niúnǎi	Milk	دودھ	نیو نائی	Du'dh
盐	Yán	Salt	نمک	یان	Neemak
糖	Táng	Sugar	چینی	تھانگ	Cheeni
大米	Dàmǐ	Rice	چاول	تامی	Chawal
面粉	Miànfěn	Wheat flour	آٹا	میان فین	Atta
酸牛奶	Suānniúnǎi	Yoghurt	دہی	سُوآن یونائی	Dahee

Lesson-20

Vocabulary - لغت , Shēngcí ,
词汇 Lu'ghut

Chinese	Pinyin	English	اُردو	چینی تلفظ	Roman Urdu
变成(变更)	Biàn chéng (biàngēng)	To become (change)	بدلنا	پیان ٹھنگ	Badalna
变化	Biànhuà	Change	تبدیلی	پیان خوآ	Tabdili
标语	Biāoyǔ	Slogan	نعرہ	پیاؤ وِی	Na'ara
表演	Biǎoyǎn	Perform	اداکاری کرنا	پیاؤ یان	Adakari-Karna
别	Bié	Do not	ہرگز نہیں	پِی ے	Hargiz Naheen
别的	Bié de	Others	دوسرے	پِی یدا	Dusre
病	Bìng	Illness	بیمار ہونا	پِینگ (لا)	Bimar Hona
博物馆	Bówùguǎn	Museum	عجائب گھر	پُو و کُو آن	Aja'ibGhar
不错	Bùcuò	Not bad	مناسب	پُو تسُوو	Munsib/ theek
布（棉）	Bù (mián)	Cloth (cotton)	کپڑا (سُوتی)	پُو (میاآن)	Kapra Suti
部	Bù	Depart-ment (bureau)	شعبہ	پُو	Sho'ba
菜（中国）	Cài (zhōng-guó)	Menu (Chinese)	کھانا (چینی)	صائی (چونگوآ)	Khana Cheeni
菜单	Càidān	Menu card	مینو کارڈ	صائی تان	Menu Card
参观	Cānguān	To visit	دورہ کرنا	صان کُوآن	Do'ra Karna

Chinese	Pinyin	English	اُردو	چینی تلفظ	Roman Urdu
参加	Cānjiā	To attend	حصہ لینا	صان چِیا	Hi'sa Lena
餐厅	Cāntīng	Restaurant	طعام گاہ	صان تھنگ	To'am Gah
草	Cǎo	Grass	گھاس	صاؤ	Gh'as
楼面	Lóu miàn	Floor	منزل (پہلی)	منگ (پہلی)	Manzil Pahli
茶	Chá	Tea	چائے	چھا	Cha'ei
差不多	Chàbùduō	Nearly	تقریباً	چھا بُو دوآ	Taqri-ban
常（常）	Cháng (cháng)	Often (very)	اکثر	چھانگ (چھانگ)	A'am Tor
唱（歌）	Chàng (gē)	Sing (song)	گانا (گانا)	چھانگ کر	Gana gana
长城	Chángchéng	Great wall	دیوار چین	چھانگ چھنگ	Diwar Cheen

Lesson-21

Vocabulary -۱ لغت , Shēngcí ، 词汇 Lu'ghut

Chinese	Pinyin	English	اُردو	چینی تلفظ	Roman Urdu
爱	Ài (verb)	Love	محبت کرنا	آئے	Muhabat karna
爱人	Àirén	Wife/ husband	بیوی یا شوہر	آئی رین	Beewi/ Shauhar
阿姨	Āyí	Aunt	چچی	آئی	Chachee
安静	Ānjìng	Quiet	خاموشی	آن چینگ	Khamooshi
暗示	Ànshì	Outline	وقت پر	آن شی	Waqt Par
爸爸	Bàba	Papa	والد	بابا	Wa'lid
白	Bái	White	سفید	پاآئی	Sufaid
百	Bǎi	Hundred	ایک سو	پاآئی	Ek Sou
半	Bàn	Half	آدھا	پانڑ	Adha
方法	Fāngfǎ	Way/ Method	طریقہ / حل	فانگ فا	Hal/Tariqa
办公室	Bàngōngshì	Office	دفتر	پان کونگ شر	Daftar
半日	Bànrì	Half day	آدھا دن	پن ری	Adha Din
帮助	Bāngzhù	Help	مدد کرنا	پانگ چُو	Madad Karna
保证	Bǎozhèng	To ensure	یقین کرنا	پاؤ ژنگ	Yaqeen Karna
报告	Bàogào	Report	اطلاع کرنا	پاؤ کاؤ	Itla Karna

Chinese	Pinyin	English	اُردو	چینی تلفظ	Roman Urdu
报纸	Bàozhǐ	Newspa-per	اخبار	پاؤ ٹر	Ikh'bar
杯子	Bēizi	Cup	پیالا	پے ذہ	Piyaala
北	Běi	North	شمال	پےاِی	Shu'mal
北京	Běijīng	Peking	بیجنگ	پے چنگ	Beijing
本子	Běnzi	Notebook	نوٹ بک	پین ذہ	Notebook
比较	Bǐjiào	Compara-tively	مقابلہ کرنا	پی چیاؤ	Muqabla karna
比赛	Bǐsài	Competi-tion	میچ	پی سا ئی	Ma'ach
必须	Bìxū	Must	ضروری	پی شوئی	Zaroori
毕业	Bìyè (verb)	To Gradu-ate	گریجویٹ	پی ے	Graduate karna

Lesson-22

Vocabulary - لغت , Shēngcí ، 词汇 Lu'ghut

Chinese	Pinyin	English	اُردو	چینی تلفظ	Roman Urdu
车	Chē	Bus	بس	ٹھِ	Bus
汽车	Qìchē	Car	گاڑی	ٹھ (چھی)	Ga'ree
车站	Chēzhàn	Bus station	بس اسٹیشن	تھ ٹر آن	Bus Station
成功	Chénggōng	Successful	کامیاب	ٹھنگ کونگ	Kamyab
成就	Chéngjiù	Achieve-ment	کامیابی	ٹھنگ چِیو	Kamy- yabi
成立	Chénglì	Establish	قاءم کرنا	ٹھنگ لِی	Qa'em Karna
产品	Chǎnpǐn	Product	اشیاء	ٹھان پھین	Ash'ya
城市(北京)	Chéngshì (běijīng)	City (Pe-king)	شہر (بیجنگ)	ٹھنگ شِی	ShaharBei-jing
成长	Chéng-zhǎng	Grow	بڑا ہونا	ٹھنگ چانگ	Bara Hona
吃	Chī	Eat	کھانا	ٹھِر	Khana
初	Chū	Beginning	شروع	ٹھو	Shuru
出发	Chūfā	Set out	روانہ کرنا	ٹھو فا	Rawana-Karna
厨房	Chúfáng	Kitchen	باورچی خانہ	ٹھو فانگ	Bawarc- hi khana
厨师	Chúshī	Cook	باورچی	ٹھو شِی	Bawar-chi

Chinese	Pinyin	English	اُردو	چینی تلفظ	Roman Urdu
穿	Chuān	Wear	پہننا	ٹھوآن	Pehanna
窗户	Chuānghù	Window	کھڑکی	ٹھوآن خو	Khirki
床	Chuáng	Bed	بستر	ٹھو آنگ	Beestar
春节	Chūnjié	Spring Festival	جشِن بہاراں	ٹھوئن چیئے	Jashn-Ba-haran
春天	Chūntiān	Spring	بہار	ٹھوئن تھیان	Ba'haar
村子	Cūnzi	Village	گاؤں	صوئن ذہ	Ga'on
错误	Cuòwù	Mistake	غلطی	صُوو	Ghalti

Lesson-23

Vocabulary - لغت , Shēngcí , 词汇 Lu'ghut

Chinese	Pinyin	English	اُردو	چینی تلفظ	Roman Urdu
打	Dǎ	To beat	مارنا	تا آ	Ma'arna
打球	Dǎqiú	Playball	گیند کھیلنا	تا آچھیُو	Ge'nd Khe'Ina
打扫	Dǎsǎo	Sweep	جھاڑو دینا	تا آساؤ	Jharoo De'na
打针	Dǎzhēn	Injection	انجیکشن	تا آڑین	Injection
大	Dà	Big	بڑا	تا	Ba'rra
大概	Dàgài	About	تقریباً	تاکائے	Takreeban
大家	Dàjiā	Everyone	ہر کوئی	تا چِیا	Har Koi
大爷	Dàyé	Eldest uncle	تا یا	تائے	Taya
大妈	Dàmā	Eldest aunt	تائی	تائی	Tayi
大使馆	Dàshǐ guǎn	Embassy	سفارتخانہ	تاشی کُوآن	Sefarat Khana
大约	Dàyuē	Nearly	اندازہ	تایوائے	Andaza
带着	Dàizhe	To take	لے کر	تائے ڑ	Le kar
代表	Dàibiǎo	Delegate	نمائندہ	تائی پیاؤ	Numainda
代表团	Dàibiǎo tuán	Delegation	وفد	تائی پیاؤ ٹھوآن	Wafd

Chinese	Pinyin	English	اُردو	چینی تلفظ	Roman Urdu
但是	Dànshì	But	لیکن	تان شی	Le'kin
当时候	Dāng shíhou	At that time	عین اس وقت	تانگ شی ہو	Ai'n Waqt
挡住	Dǎngzhù	To block	روکنا	تانگ چُو	Rokna
刀	Dāo	Knife	چھری	تاو	Chu'uri
到	Dào	To arrive	پہنچنا	تاوٗ	Pahunchna
道理	Dàolǐ	Reason	وجہ	تاوٗلی	Wa'jah
得到	Dédào	To get	حاصل کرنا	دَ تاوٗ	Hasil Karna
等	Děng	To wait	انتظار کرنا	تنگ	Intezar

Lesson-24

Vocabulary - لغت , Shēngcí ,
词汇 Lu'ghut

Chinese	Pinyin	English	اُردو	چینی تلفظ	Roman Urdu
低	Dī	Low	نیچا	تِی	Neecha
敌人	Dírén	Enemy	دشمن	تِی رِین	Dush-man
抵抗	Dǐkàng	To resist	مُزاحمت کرنا	تِی کھانگ	Muzahmat Karna
弟弟	Dìdì	Younger brother	چھوٹا بھائی	تِی دی	Chota Bhai
地方	Dìfāng	Place	جگہ	تِی فانگ	Jaga'h
地图	Dìtú	Map	نقشہ	تِی تھو	Naqsha
点	Diǎn	Little (a)	تھوڑا سا	ڈیانر (اِی)	Thora sa
电报	Diànbào	Telegram	ٹیلیگرام	تیان پاؤ	Telegram
灯	Dēng	Light	روشنی	تنگ	Roshni
电	Diàn	Electric	بجلی	تیان	Beejli
电站	Diànzhàn	Power project	بجلی گھر	تیان ٹر آن	Beejli Ghar
电话	Diànhuà	Telephone	ٹیلی فون	تیان خو آ	Telephone
电话（手机）	Diànhuà (shǒujī)	Mobile phone	مو باءل فون	تیان خو آ (شَوچی)	Mobile Phone
电视	Diànshì	Television	ٹی وی	تیان شی	T.V

Chinese	Pinyin	English	اُردو	چینی تلفظ	Roman Urdu
电影	Diànyǐng	Movie/film	فلم	تِیان اِینگ	Film
电影管	Diànyǐng guǎn	Cinema	سینما	تِیان اِینگ گو آن	Cinema
订（票）	Dìng (piào)	Book (ticket)	بُکنگ	تینگ (پھیاؤ)	Booking
丢	Diū	To lose	ہارنا	تِی یو	Har'na
东方	Dōngfāng	East	مشرق	تونگ فانگ	Mashriq
冬天	Dōngtiān	Winter	موسم سرما	تونگ تھیان	Mausim Sarma
懂	Dǒng le	Understood	سمجھ (لیا)	تونگ (لا)	Samjh lia
都	Dōu	All	سب	طو	Sab/Sa're
读	Dú	To read	پڑھنا	ٹو	Par'hna

Lesson-25

Vocabulary - لغت , Shēngcí , 词汇 Lu'ghut

Chinese	Pinyin	English	اُردو	چینی تلفظ	Roman Urdu
独立	Dúlì	Indepen-dence	آزادی	ٹولی	Azadi
短	Duǎn	Short	چھوٹا	ٹوآن	Chota
锻炼	Duànliàn	Exercise	ورزش کرنا	ٹو آن لِیان	Warzish Karna
对	Duì	Right/OK	صحیح / ٹھیک	ٹوئی	Theek/Sa-hee
对不起	Duìbùqǐ	Sorry	معافی کا طلبگار	ٹوئی پُو چھِی	Ma'fee Ka Izha'ar
多少	Duōshǎo	How much	کتنا	ٹووشاؤ	Ke'tna
多	Duō	More	زیادہ	ٹوو	Ziya'ada
多吗	Duō ma	How many	کتنا	ٹو وما	Ke'tna
饿	È	Hungry	بُھوکا	غَہ (لا)	Bhu'uka
而且	Érqiě	But also	بلکہ	اَر چھے	Bal'ke
儿子	Érzi	Son	بیٹا	اَرضہ	Be'ta
发表	Fābiǎo	Publish	شاءع کرنا	فاپیاؤ	Sha'ey Karna
发达	Fādá	Developed	ترقی یافتہ	فا تا	Tarraqi Yafta
发电机	Fādiàn jī	Electric generator	بجلی جنریٹر	فاتِیانجی	Bijli gener-ator

Chinese	Pinyin	English	اُردو	چینی تلفظ	Roman Urdu
发给	Fā gěi	To issue	رسید دینا	فآکے اِی	Raseed Lena
发明	Fāmíng	Invention	ایجاد کرنا	فآمِینگ	E'jad Karna
发烧	Fāshāo	Have fever	بخار ہونا	فآ شَا وَ	Bukhar Hona
发生	Fāshēng	To happen/ occur	واقع پزیر ہونا	فآشنگ	Waq'ye pazir Hona
发现	Fāxiàn	To find/ discover	معلوم/ دریافت کرنا	فآشیان	Daryaft/ MalumKar-na
发展	Fāzhǎn	To develop	ترقی کرنا	فآژان	Tarraqi Karna
翻译	Fānyì	To trans-late	ترجمہ کرنا	فآن اِی	Tarjuma Karna

Lesson-26

Vocabulary - لغت , Shēngcí ,
词汇 Lu'ghut

Chinese	Pinyin	English	اُردو	چینی تلفظ	Roman Urdu
反对	Fǎnduì	To oppose	مخالفت کرنا	فآن تُو ئی	Mukhalfat Karna
反对派	Fǎnduì pài	Opposition party	حِزب مخالف	فآن تُوئی پھاے	Hizb Mukhalif
防抗	Fáng kàng	To resist	مزاحمت کرنا	فآن کھانگ	Muzahm-mat karna
饭	Fàn	Rice	چاول	فَن (ی)	Chawal
饭馆	Fànguǎn	Restaurant	ریسٹوران	فَن کنواڑ	Resturant
方便	Fāngbiàn	Convenient	آسانی	فانگ پیان	Asaani
方面	Fāngmiàn	Aspect	زاویہ	فانگ مِیان	Zawiya
房间	Fángjiān	Room	کمرہ	فانگ چیان	Kamra
房子	Fángzi	House	گھر	فانگ ذہ	Ghar
访问	Fǎngwèn	To visit	دورہ کرنا	فانگ وین	DorahKar-na
放假	Fàngjià	Holiday	چُھٹی	فانگ چِیا	Chu'tti
飞	Fēi	To fly	اُڑنا	فے اِی	Urna
非常	Fēicháng	Very much	بہت زیادہ	فیٹھا نگ	Bahut Ziyadah
肥皂	Féizào	Soap	صابن	فِیذاؤ	Sab'un

Chinese	Pinyin	English	اُردو	چینی تلفظ	Roman Urdu
分	Fēn	Cent	پیسہ	فِین	Paisa
分（钟）	Fēn (zhōng)	Minute(-Time)	مِنٹ	فِین (چونگ)	Mint Waqt
奋斗	Fèndòu	To struggle	جدوجہد کرنا	فین تو	Jido Jahd Karna
丰富	Fēngfù	Rich	بہت زیادہ	فنگ فُو	Bahot Ziada
丰富（文化）	Fēngfù (wénhuà)	Rich culture	شاندار ثقافتی روایت	فنگ فو (وین خو آ)	Shandar Saqafati Riwayat
风景（美丽）	Fēngjǐng (měilì)	Scenery (Beautiful)	خوبصورت منظر	فنگ چینگ (میلِی)	Khub Surat Manzar
丰收（小麦）	Fēngshōu (xiǎomài)	Bumper harvest	وافر پیداوار	فنگ شوشیاؤ مائی	Wafir Paydawar
服务（员）	Fúwù (yuán)	To service	خدمت کرنا (ملازم)	فو اوٗ (یو آن)	Khidmat Karna
附近	Fùjìn	Near	قریب	فُو چِن	Qareeb
复杂	Fùzá	Complicated	پیچیدہ	فوزا	Pechida
反对	Fǎnduì	Oppose	مخالفت کرنا	فان توی	Mukh-Alfat Karna

Lesson-27

Vocabulary - لغت , Shēngcí , 词汇 Lu'ghut

Chinese	Pinyin	English	اُردو	چینی تلفظ	Roman Urdu
干净	Gānjìng	Clean	صاف ستھرا	کان چینگ	Saf Suthra
感动	Gǎndòng	Moved	متاثر ہونا	کاآن تونگ	Mut'sir Karna
赶快	Gǎnkuài	Quickly	جلدی	کاآن کھوآئی	Jaldi
感冒	Gǎnmào	Cold/flu	نزلہ وزکام ہونا	کاآن ماؤ (لا)	Nazla-zu-kam
感谢	Gǎnxiè	To thank	شکریہ	کاآن شیے	Shukrya
干（活）	Gàn (huó)	To work	کام کرنا	کان (خور)	Kam Karna
公仆	Gōngpú	Public servant	سرکاری ملازم	کان پُو	Sarkari Mulazim
钢	Gāng	Steel	اسٹیل	کانگ	Steel
钢笔	Gāngbǐ	Pen	قلم	کانگ پی	Qalam
刚才	Gāngcái	Just now	ابھی ابھی	کانگ ضاے	Abhi-abhi
高	Gāo	High	اونچا	کاؤ	U'ncha
高兴	Gāoxìng	Happy	خوش	کاو شِنگ	Khoosh
告诉	Gàosu	To tell	اطلاع دینا	کاو سُو	I'tla dena
哥哥	Gēgē	Elder brother	بڑا بھائی	کہ گا	Bara bhai

Chinese	Pinyin	English	اُردو	چینی تلفظ	Roman Urdu
歌	Gē	Song	گانا	کر	Gana
革命	Gémìng	Revolution	انقلاب	کہ مِنگ	Inqilab
（一）个	Gè (yī)	One item	ایک عدد	گہ (اِی)	Ek Adad
（每）个	Gè (měi)	Every item	ہر کوئی	گہ (مے)	Har Koi
给	Gěi	To give	دینا	کے اِی	Dena
跟	Gēn	With	ساتھ	کین	Sath
更（多	Gēn (duō)	More	زیادہ	کنگ ٹُو و	Ziyadah
工厂	Gōngchǎng	Factory	کارخانہ	کونگ ٹھانگ	Karkhana

Lesson-28

Vocabulary - لغت , Shēngcí ، 词汇 Lu'ghut

Chinese	Pinyin	English	اُردو	چینی تلفظ	Roman Urdu
工程师	Gōngchéng-shī	Engineer	انجنیر	کونگٹھنگ شی	Engineer
公里	Gōnglǐ	Kilometer	کلومیٹر	کونگ لی	Kilometer
工人	Gōngrén	Worker	مزدور	کونگ رین	Mazdoor
工业	Gōngyè	Industry	صنعت	کونگ یے	Se'naat
公元	Gōngyuán	B.C (Birth of Christ)	عیسوی	کونگ یُوآن	Iswee
工作	Gōngzuò	To work	کام کرنا	کونگ ذواو	Kam Karna
共产党	Gòngc-hǎndǎng	Commu-nist Party	کمیونسٹ پارٹی	کونگ ٹھان تانگ	Communist Party
共和国	Gònghéguó	Republic	جمہوریہ	کونگ خاکُوآ	Jamhuriya
贡献	Gòngxiàn	Contribu-tion	حصہ	کونگ شیان	His'sa
姑娘	Gūniang	Girl	لڑکی	کُونیانگ	Larki
古	Gǔ	Ancient	قدیم	کُو	Qadeem
古代	Gǔdài	Ancient	قدیم	کُوتائی	Qadeem
古迹	Gǔjī	Historical site	تاریخی مقامات	کُوچی	Tareekh-iMuka-ma'at
鼓励	Gǔlì	To encour-age	ہمت افزائی	کُولی	Himat-e-Afzai

Chinese	Pinyin	English	اُردو	چینی تلفظ	Roman Urdu
故宫	Gùgōng	Imperial Palace	اِمپریل پیلس	گُوکونگ	Imperial Palace
客户	Kèhù	Customer	خریدار	کُوکھ	Khareedar
故事	Gùshì	Story	کہانی	گُوشی	Kaha'ani
关	Guān	To close	بند کرنا	گوآن	Bund Karna
灌溉	Guàngài	To irrigate	آبپاشی کرنا	گُوآن کاے	Abpashi-Karna
广州	Guǎngzhōu	Canton	کینٹن	گوانگ چو	Canton
贵	Guì	Expensive	مہنگا	گُوئی	Meh'nga
国	Guó	Country	ملک	گوآو	Mulk
国家	Guójiā	Country	ملک	گوآوچیا	Mulk

Lesson-29

Vocabulary - لغت , Shēngcí , 词汇 Lu'ghut

Chinese	Pinyin	English	اُردو	چینی تلفظ	Roman Urdu
国际	Guójì	Interna-tional	بین القوامی	گُووجِی	Ban-ul-Aqwami
国际主义	Guójì zhǔyì	Interna-tionalism	بین القوامیت	گُووجِی جُوئی	Ban-ul-aqwamit
过	Guò	To spend	گزارہ کرنا	گُوو	Guzarah-Karna
还	Hái	Still	زیادہ	ہائی	Ziyadha
还是	Háishì	Or	یا	ہائی شی	Ya
孩子	Háizi	Child	بچہ	ہائی زہ	Bachha
海	Hǎi	Sea	سمندر	ہاآئی	Samundar
害	Hài	To harm	نقصان پہنچانا	ہائی	Nuqsan Pa-hunchana
害怕	Hàipà	To fear	ڈرنا	ہائی پھا	Darna
喊	Hǎn	To shout	چیخنا	ہاآن	Cheekhna
汉语	Hànyǔ	Chinese	چینی	خانوِی	Cheeni
汉字	Hànzì	Chinese character	چینی حروف	خانزی	Cheeni Huruf
好	Hǎo	Fine	اچھا	خاؤ	Ach'aa
好看	Hǎokàn	Pretty	خوبصورت	خاؤکھن	Khubsurat

Chinese	Pinyin	English	اُردو	چینی تلفظ	Roman Urdu
好了	Hǎole	All right	ٹھک ہے	خاولا	Theek Hai
号码	Hàomǎ	Number	عدد	خاو	Adad
喝	Hé	To drink	پینا	خہ	Peena
和	Hé	And	اور	خا	Aur
河	Hé	River	دریا	خا	Darya
和平	Hépíng	Peace	امن	خاپھنگ	Aman
很（好）	Hěn (hǎo)	Very (good)	بہت اچھا	خین خاو	Bahut Ach’aa
很厚	Hěn hòu	Thick	موٹا	خُو	Motta
后来	Hòulái	Later on	بعد میں	خو لائی	Ba’ad me
胡同	Hútòng	Lane	گلی	خُو تھونگ	Galee

Lesson-30

Vocabulary - لغت , Shēngcí ، 词汇 Lu'ghut

Chinese	Pinyin	English	اُردو	چینی تلفظ	Roman Urdu
互相	Hùxiāng	Mutual	باہمی	خُوشیانگ	Bah'mi
花	Huā	Flower	پھول	خُوار	Phool
花束	Huāshù	Bouquet	گُلدستہ	خُواشُو	Guldasta
画	Huà	To draw	مصوری کرنا	خُوآ	Musawari Karna
话剧	Huàjù	Play	ڈرامہ	خُوچُوئی	Darama
坏了	Huàile	To become bad	خراب ہونا	خوآئی (لہ)	Kharab Hona
欢乐	Huānlè	Happiness	خوشی	خوآن لہ	Khuushi
欢送	Huānsòng	To send off	الوداع کرنا	خوان سونگ	Alweeda Karna
欢迎	Huānyíng	To wel-come	خوش آمدید کرنا	خوان یِنگ	Khush Am-ded Karna
换（钱）	Huàn (qián)	To change (money)	زرمبادلہ	خُوان (چھیان)	Zarme Mubadla
恢复	Huīfù	To restore	بحال کرنا	خُوئی فو	Bahal Karna
回	Huí	To return	واپس ہونا	خُوئی	Wapas Hona
回答	Huídá	To answer	جواب دینا	خوئی تا	Jawab Dena
活	Huó	To live	زندہ رہنا	خُوو	Zinda Rahna

Chinese	Pinyin	English	اُردو	چینی تلفظ	Roman Urdu
获得	Huòdé	To obtain	حاصل کرنا	خوودا	Hasil Karna
火	Huǒ	Fire	آگ	خُوو	A'agh
火车	Huǒchē	Train	ریل گاڑی	خُووچھا	Rail Garee
火车站	Huǒchē zhàn	Train station	ٹرین اسٹیشن	خووچھاڑآن	Rail Station

Lesson-31

Vocabulary - لغت , Shēngcí，词汇 Lu'ghut

Chinese	Pinyin	English	اُردو	چینی تلفظ	Roman Urdu
几（个）	Jǐ (gè)	How (many)	کتنی/کتنا	چی (گہ)	Ketna/ Ketni
季（春）	Jì (chūn)	(Spring) season	موسم (بہار)	چی (ٹھوئن)	Mausim/ Bahar
寄	Jì	To mail	ڈاک سے بھیجنا	چی	Dak se Bhejna
记	Jì	To remember	یاد کرنا	چی	Yad Karna
计划	Jìhuà	To plan	ہدف بنانا	چی خوآ	Hadaf Banana
机会	Jīhuì	Opportunity	موقع	چی خُوئی	Mo'qaa
积极	Jījí	Active	مُستعد	چی چِی	Musta'ad
激烈	Jīliè	Exciting	ولولہ انگیز	چی لیے	Walwal'Angez
机器	Jīqì	Machinery	مشین	چی چھی	Machinery
激动	Jīdòng	Moved by	پُر اثر ہونا	چی ڈونگ	Pur'asr hona
纪念	Jìniàn	To celebrate	جشن منانا	چی نیان	Jashn manana
继续	Jìxù	To continue	جاری رکھنا	چی شُوئی	Jaree Rakhna
坚持	Jiānchí	To persevere	ثابت قدمی	چیان تھِر	Saabit Qadmi
坚决	Jiānjué	Firmly	عزم	چیان چُولے	Azam

Chinese	Pinyin	English	اُردو	چینی تلفظ	Roman Urdu
艰苦	Jiānkǔ	Hard work	سخت محنت	چیان کھو	Sakht Mehnat
坚强	Jiānqiáng	Strong	مضبوط	چیان چھیانگ	Mazboot
监狱	Jiānyù	Prison	جیل	چیان ایوی	Jail
简单	Jiǎndān	Simple	سادہ	چیان دان	Sa'daah
见	Jiàn	To see	دیکھنا	چیان	Dekhna
建设	Jiànshè	To build	تعمیر کرنا	چِیان شِی	Ta'meer karna
建筑	Jiànzhú	Building	عمارت	چیان ٹو	Emarat
将来	Jiānglái	Future	مستقبل	چیانگ لاے	Mustaqbil
讲	Jiǎng	To speak	بولنا	چیانگ	Bolna

Lesson-32

Vocabulary - لغت , Shēngcí ,
词汇 Lu'ghut

Chinese	Pinyin	English	اُردو	چینی تلفظ	Roman Urdu
郊区	Jiāoqū	Neighbour-hood	مضافات	چیاو چھوئی	Mu'zaafat
教书	Jiāoshū	To teach	درس دینا	چیاو شو	Dars dena
交谈	Jiāotán	Consulta-tion	مذاکرات	چیاو تھان	Muzakarat
交友	Jiāoyǒu	Picnic	پکنک	چیاو یو	Picnic
脚	Jiǎo	Foot	پیر	چیاو	Pair
叫	Jiào	Called	پکارنا (نام)	چیاو (منگزہ)	Pukarna
教师	Jiàoshī	Teacher	اُستاد	چیاو شی	Ustad
教育	Jiàoyù	Education	تعلیم	چیاو ایوی	Taa'leem
接待	Jiēdài	To receive	خاطر مدارت کرنا	چیے تائی	Khatir Madarat karna
街道	Jiēdào	Street	سڑک	چے تاو	Sarak
接过	Jiēguò	To take over	سنبھال لینا	چے کُوو	Sambhal lena
结果	Jiéguǒ	Result	نتیجہ	چے کُوآ	Nateeja
节目	Jiémù	Program	پروگرام	چے مُو	Program
节日	Jiérì	Holiday	چُھٹی	چے ری	Chutthi

Chinese	Pinyin	English	اُردو	چینی تلفظ	Roman Urdu
结束	Jiéshù	End	ختم ہونا	جے شُو	Khatam Hona
解放	Jiěfàng	To liberate	آزاد ہونا	جے فانگ	Azad hona
解决	Jiějué	To solve	حل کرنا	جے جُوے	Hal Karna
介绍	Jièshào	To intro-duce	تعارف کرنا	جے شاو	Ta'aruf Karna
近	Jìn	Near	نزدیک	جِن	Nazdeek
进	Jìn	To enter	داخل ہونا	جِن	Dakhil hona
进步	Jìnbù	Progress	ترقی	جِینپو	Taraqqi
进行	Jìnxíng	To carry out	جاری رکھنا	جِن شِنگ	Jaari Ra-khna
精彩	Jīngcǎi	Excellent	اعلیٰ	جِنگ صائی	A'ala
Chinese	Pinyin	English	اُردو	تلفظ	Roman Urdu
精神	Jīngshén	Spirit	جذبہ	جِنگ شِین	Jazba
旧	Jiù	Old	پُرانا	جِیو	Pu'rana
觉得	Juéde	To feel	احساس کرنا	جِوے دا	Ehsas Karna
军队	Jūnduì	Army	فوج	جِوءِن تُوئی	Fauj

Lesson-33

Vocabulary - لغت , Shēngcí ,
词汇 Lu'ghut

Chinese	Pinyin	English	اُردو	چینی تلفظ	Roman Urdu
开（门）	Kāi (mén)	Open (door)	کھولنا (دروازہ)	کھائی (مین)	Kholna Darwaza
开始	Kāishǐ	To begin	آغاز کرنا/ شروع	کھائی شی	Aghaz/ Shruu Karna
开水	Kāishuǐ	Boiled water	گرم پانی	کھائی شوئی	Garm Paani
开（晚会）	Kāi (wǎn-huì)	To hold a meeting	میٹینگ کرنا	کھائی (وآن خوئی)	Meeting-Karna
开（玩笑）	Kāi (wánx-iào)	To make a joke	ہنسی مزاق کرنا	کھائی وآن شیاو	Ha'nsee Mazaq Karna
看	Kàn	To look	دیکھنا	کھَن	Dekhna
看（病）	Kàn (bìng)	To look for (doc-tor)	ڈاکٹر سے رجوع کرنا	کھَن (پینگ)	Doctor se Ruju Karna
看见	Kànjiàn	Saw	دیکھا	کھَن چیان	Dekha
可（了）	Kě (le)	Thirst (have)	پیاس (ہونا)	کھہ (لا)	Piyas Hona
可靠	Kěkào	Reliable	بااعتماد	کھہ کھاو	Ba'Ite-mad
可怜	Kělián	To pity	ہمدردی کرنا	کھہ لیان	Hamdar-di
可是	Kěshì	But	لیکن	کھِہ شی	Le'kin

Chinese	Pinyin	English	اُردو	چینی تلفظ	Roman Urdu
可以（了）	Kěyǐ (le)	Ok (Is)	ٹھیک (ہے)	کھ ایلا	Theek Hai
克服	Kèfú	To over-come	قابو کرنا	کھ فو	Qabu Karna
客气	Kèqì	Polite	شائستگی	کھ چھی	Shae'sta-gi
客人	Kèrén	Guest	مہمان	کھ ریَن	Mehman
口	Kǒu	Mouth	منہ	کھوو	Mun'h
口袋	Kǒudài	Sack (Pocket)	تھیلا (پاکٹ)	کھو تائی	Thee'la
哭	Kū	To cry	رونا	کھُو	Rona
苦	Kǔ	Bitter	تیز ذائقہ	کھُوو	Tez Zaiqa
裤子	Kùzi	Trouser	پینٹ	کھُوزہ	Pe't
快	Kuài	Quickly	تیز (جلدی)	کھُوآئی	Tez
宽	Kuān	Spacious (wide)	کُشادہ	کھُوان	Kushada
困难	Kùnnán	Difficult	مشکل	کھُوءنان	Mushkil

Lesson-34

Vocabulary - لغت , Shēngcí ,
词汇 Lu'ghut

Chinese	Pinyin	English	اُردو	چینی تلفظ	Roman Urdu
来了	Láile	Has come	آیا	لائی لا	Ae'yaa
来源	Láiyuán	Source	زریعہ	لائی یو آن	Zarya
篮球	Lánqiú	Basketball	باسکٹ بال	لان چِھیو	Basketball
狼	Láng	Wolf	بھیڑیا	لانگ	Bher'iya
劳动	Láodòng	To work	محنت کرنا	لاو تونگ	Mehnat Karna
老	Lǎo	Old	بوڑھا	لا آو	Burha
老大爷	Lǎo dàyé	Elder uncle	بڑے ابا	لاوتاے	Bare Abba
老师	Lǎoshī	Teacher	استاد / استانی	لاو شِی	Ustani/ Ustad
老头子	Lǎotóuzi	Old man	بوڑھا آدمی	لاو تھاوذہ	Burha Admi
累（了）	Lèi (le)	(get) Tired	تھک (گیا)	لے ایلا	Thak Gaya
冷	Lěng	Cold	ٹھنڈک	لَنگ	Thandak
里（一）	Lǐ (yī)	Half kilometre	نصف کلومیٹر	لی (اِی)	Nisf Kilo-meter
里（边）	Lǐ (biān)	Inside	اندر	لی پیان	Under
理发	Lǐfǎ	Haircut	حجامت بنانا	لی فا	Hijamat Karna

Chinese	Pinyin	English	اُردو	چینی تلفظ	Roman Urdu
理发院	Lǐfǎ yuàn	Barber shop	حجام	لی فایو آن	Hijam
理论	Lǐlùn	Theory	اصول (نظریہ)	لی لوءن	Usool
礼物	Lǐwù	Gift	تحفہ	لیوو	Tuhfa
立刻	Lìkè	Immediately	فوراً	لی کھ	For'an
力量	Lìliàng	Strength	طاقت	لی لیانگ	Ta'qat
力气	Lìqì	Strength	طاقت	لی چھی	Ta'qat
例如	Lìrú	Example	مثال	لی رو	Mee'sal
历史	Lìshǐ	History	تاریخ	لی شی	Tareekh
连接	Liánjiē	To connect	جوڑنا	لیان چِے	Jorna
联系	Liánxì	Contact	رابطہ کرنا	لِیان شی	Rabta Karna
脸	Liǎn	Face	چہرہ	لیاآن	Chehra

Lesson-35

Vocabulary - لغت , Shēngcí , 词汇 Lu'ghut

Chinese	Pinyin	English	اُردو	چینی تلفظ	Roman Urdu
练习	Liànxí	Exercise	مشق	لِیان شی	Mashq
凉	Liáng	Cool	ٹھنڈہ	لیانگ	Thanda
粮食	Liángshí	Grain	اناج	لیانگ شی	Anaj
了解	Liǎojiě	To find out	پتہ کرنا	لیاو چے	Pata Karna
临（时）	Lín (shí)	About (time)	عین (وقت)	لِین شی	Ain Waqt
邻居	Línjū	Neighbour	پڑوسی	لِین چُوئی	Parrosi
邻（国）	Lín (guó)	Neighbouring country	پڑوسی ملک	لِین گُوو	Parrosi Mulk
零件	Língjiàn	Spare parts	اسپیر پارٹ	لِنگ چیان	Spare parts
领	Lǐng	To lead	رہنمائی کرنا	لینگ	Rahnumai Karna
领导	Lǐngdǎo	Leadership	قیادت	لینگ (تاو)	Qiyadat
领袖	Lǐngxiù	Leader	رہنما	لینگ شِیو	Rahnuma
另外	Lìngwài	Other than	علاوہ ازین	لینگ وائی	Elawa Azin
离开	Líkāi	To leave	روانہ ہونا	لی کھائے	Rawana Hona
流利	Liúlì	Fluently	روانی سے	لِیُو لی	Rawani se

Chinese	Pinyin	English	اردو	چینی تلفظ	Roman Urdu
楼(大)	lóu(Dà)	Building	عمارت (بلاک)	لاؤ	Emarat Block
楼上	lóu shàng	Upstairs	اوپر منزل	لوشیانگ	Upar Manzil
楼下	Lóu xià	Downstairs	نچلی منزل	لوشیا	Nichli Man-zil
路	Lù	Road	سڑک	لُو	Sarak
驴	Lǘ	Donkey	گدھا	لو	Gad'haa
旅馆	Lǚguǎn	Hotel	ہوٹل	لُوئی کوآن	Hotel
旅行	lǚxíng	To travel	سفر کرنا	لوئی شِینگ	Safar Karna
乱	Luàn	Chaos (Messy)	بُحران	لوآن	Buhran

Lesson-36

Vocabulary - لغت , Shēngcí , 词汇 Lu'ghut

Chinese	Pinyin	English	اُردو	چینی تلفظ	Roman Urdu
吗	Ma	Question	کیا	ما	Kiya
马	Mǎ	Horse	گھوڑا	ما	Ghorra
马路	Mǎlù	Road	سڑک	مالو	Sarr'ak
马上	Mǎshàng	Immedi-ately	فوراً	ماشنگ	Fo'run
买	Mǎi	To buy	خریدنا	مائی	Khareedna
卖	Mài	To sell	فروخت کرنا	ماءِی	Farokht Karna
馒头	Mántou	Steamed roll	چینی رول	مان تھو	Cheeni Roll
慢	Màn	Slowly	آہستہ	ماِن	Ahista
忙	Máng	Busy	مصروف	مانگ	Masroof
毛巾	Máojīn	Towel	تولیہ	ماو چِن	To'liya
毛衣	Máoyī	Sweater	سوءٹر	ماو اِی	Sweater
帽子	Màozi	Hat	ٹوپی	ماو زہ	Topi
没关系	Méiguānxì	Never mind	کوئی بات نہیں	مے کو آن شی	Koi Bat Nahee
没有	Méiyǒu	Do not (have)	نہیں (ہے)	مے یو	Nahee hai

Chinese	Pinyin	English	اُردو	چینی تلفظ	Roman Urdu
美	Měi	Beautiful	خوبصورت	مے اِی	Khub Surat
每（个）	Měi (gè)	Every	ہر ایک	مے (گہ)	Har Ek
美丽	Měilì	Pretty	حسین	مے لِی	Haseen
妹妹	Mèimei	Younger sister	چھوٹی بہن	مے مے	Choti Ba-han
闷	mèn	To suffo-cate	سانس پھولنا	مین سِی	Sans Phul-na
门	Mén	Door	دروازہ	مین	Darwaza
门口	Ménkǒu	Gate	گیٹ	مین کھو	Gate
米	Mǐ	Meter	میٹر	مِی	Meter
米饭	Mǐfàn	Rice	چاول	مِی فان	Chawal
棉花	Miánhuā	Cotton	کپاس	میان خوآ	Kap'as
免费	Miǎnfèi	Free of charge	مفت	میان فے	Muft

Lesson-37

Vocabulary - لغت , Shēngcí , 词汇 Lu'ghut

Chinese	Pinyin	English	اُردو	چینی تلفظ	Roman Urdu
面	Miàn	Flour	آٹا	مِیان	A'tta
面包	Miànbāo	Bread	ڈبل روٹی	مِیان پاؤ	Double Rotti
面条	Miàntiáo	Noodle	نوڈل	میان تھیاو	Noodle
秒（分）	Miǎo (fēn)	Second	سیکنڈ	میآو	Second
民主	Mínzhǔ	Democracy	جمہوریت	مینٹو	Jamhuriyat
民族	Mínzú	Nationality	قومیت	مینذو	Qaumiyat
明白	Míngbái	Under-stand	سمجھنا	مِینگ پائی	Samajhna
名胜	Míngshèng	Scenic spot	حسین نظارہ	مِینگ شِنگ	Haseen Nazara
明天	Míngtiān	Tomorrow	آنے والا کل	مِینگ تھیان	Ane wala Kal
名字	Míngzì	Name	نام	مِینگ ذہ	Na'am
墨水	Mòshuǐ	Ink	روشنائی	مُوشوئی	Roshnai
母亲	Mǔqīn	Mother	ماں	مُوچھین	Ma
母鸡	Mǔ jī	Hen	مرغی	مُوجِی	Murghi
哪个	Nǎge	Which (one)	کون	ناگہ	Kon

Chinese	Pinyin	English	اُردو	چینی تلفظ	Roman Urdu
哪	Nǎ	Where	کہاں	نآر	Ka'han
那个	Nàgè	That one	وہ (والا)	ناگہ	Woh(wala)
那	Nà	There	وہاں	نار	Wahan
难	Nán	Hard	سخت	نان	Sakht
南	Nán	South	جنوب	نان	Janub
男孩	Nánhái	Boy	لڑکا	نان حر	Larka
女孩	Nǚhái	Girl	لڑکی	نُواِی حر	Larki
内边	Nèi biān	Inside	اندر	نےِ پیان	Under
能	Néng	Can	سکنا	ننگ	Sakna
你	Nǐ	You	تم	نِی	Tum

Lesson-38

Vocabulary - لغت , Shēngcí ، 词汇 Lu'ghut

Chinese	Pinyin	English	اُردو	چینی تلفظ	Roman Urdu
您	Nín	You	آپ	نِین	A'ap
你们	Nǐmen	You (plural)	تُم لوگ	نِی مین	Tum Log
年	Nián	Year	سال	نِیان	Sa'al
年纪	Niánjì	Age	عمر	نِیانچی	Umar
念	Niàn	Read	پڑھنا	نِیان	Par'rhna
牛奶	Niúnǎi	Milk	دودھ	نیونائی	Du'udh
农村	Nóngcūn	Village	گاوں	نونگ سوءن	Gao'on
农夫	Nóngfū	Farmer	کسان	نونگ مین	Kisan
农业	Nóngyè	Agriculture	زراعت	نونگ ے	Zarra'at
努力	Nǔlì	Hard work	سخت محنت	نُولی	Sakht Mehnat
女儿	Nǚ'ér	Daughter	بیٹی	نااِر	Betty
暖和	Nuǎnhuo	Warm	گرم	نُوآن خوو	Garam
暖气	Nuǎnqì	Warmth	گرمی	نُوآن چھی	Garmi
爬山	Páshān	Climb	پہاڑ چڑھنا	پھاشان	Pahar Charna

Chinese	Pinyin	English	اُردو	چینی تلفظ	Roman Urdu
怕	Pà	Fear	ڈرنا	پھا	Darna
排球	Páiqiú	Volleyball	والی بال	پھائی چھیو	Volleyball
派	Pài	To send	بھیجنا	پھائی	Bhejna
旁（边）	Páng (biān)	Side	طرف	پھانگ	Taraf
跑	Pǎo	Run	بھاگنا	پھاو	Bhagna
培养	Péiyǎng	Educate	تعلیم و تربیت کرنا	پھِے یانگ	Taaleem Tarbiya
朋友	Péngyǒu	Friend	دوست	پھَنگ یو	Do'st
批评	Pīpíng	Criticize	نکتہ چینی کرنا	پھی پھِنگ	Nukta Cheeni Karna

Lesson-39

Vocabulary - لغت , Shēngcí ,
词汇 Lu'ghut

Chinese	Pinyin	English	اُردو	چینی تلفظ	Roman Urdu
皮	Pí	Fur/Skin	چمڑا	پھی	Chamra
便宜	Piányi	Cheap	سستہ	پیان اِی	Sasta
票	Piào	Ticket	ٹکٹ	پھیاو	Ticket
乒乓球	Pīngpāng qiú	Table tennis	پِنگ پانگ	پنگ پانگ چِھیو	Table tennis
瓶	Píng	Bottle	بوتل	پھینگ	Bottle
平等	Píngděng	Equal	برابر	پھینگ تنگ	Bara'bar
妻子	Qīzi	Wife	بیوی	چِھی زہ	Bee'wi
其他	Qítā	Others	دوسرا	چِھی تھا	Dusra
千	Qiān	Thousand	ہزار	چھیان	Hazar
铅笔	Qiānbǐ	Pencil	پنسل	چھیان پی	Pencil
钱	Qián	Money	روپیہ	چِھیان	Rupiah
钱包	Qiánbāo	Purse	پرس	چِھیان پاو	Purse
前（边）	Qián (biān)	Front	سامنے طرف	چِھیان (پیان)	Samne-Taraf
前进	Qiánjìn	To advance	پیش قدمی کرنا	چھیان چِن	Pesh Qad-mi Karna

Chinese	Pinyin	English	اُردو	چینی تلفظ	Roman Urdu
前面	Qiánmiàn	Front	سامنے	چھیان مِیان	Samne
前天	Qiántiān	Day before yesterday	گزشتہ کل	چھیان تھیان	Guzishta Kal
前途	Qiántú	Future	مُستقبل	چھِیان تھُو	Mustaqbil
抢	Qiǎng	Gun	بندوق	چھِیانگ	Bandooq
抢救	Qiǎngjiù	To save life	بچانا	چھِیانگ چِیو	Bachana
敲	Qiāo	Knock	دستک دینا	چھِیاو	Dastak Dena
桥梁	Qiáoliáng	Bridge	پُل	چھیاو لِیانگ	Pul

Lesson-40

Vocabulary - لغت , Shēngcí ، 词汇 Lu'ghut

Chinese	Pinyin	English	اُردو	چینی تلفظ	Roman Urdu
亲爱	Qīn'ài	Dear	محترم	چھِن آئی	Muhtaram
侵略	Qīnlüè	Aggression	جارحیت کرنا	چھِن لُوئے	Jarhiyat Karna
秦朝	Qín cháo	Qin dynas-ty	چھِن دور حکومت	چھِنگ ٹھاو	Chin DorHu-kumat
勤劳	Qínláo	Industrious	محنت کش	چھِن لاو	Mehnat Kash
清除	Qīngchú	Clear	صاف	چھِنگ ٹھو	Saaf
青年	Qīngnián	Youth	نوجوان	چھِنگ نیان	Naju'wan
情况	Qíngkuàng	Situation	حالات	چھِنگ کھوانگ	Hala'at
请	Qǐng	Please	مہربانی	چھِنگ	Meharbani
穷	Qióng	Poor	غریب	چھِیونگ	Ghareeb
秋天	Qiūtiān	Autumn	خزاں	چھِیو تھیان	Kheza'an
取得	Qǔdé	To achieve	کامیاب ہونا	چھُوئی دا	Kamyab Hona
去	Qù	To go	جانا	چھُوئی	Jana
去年	Qùnián	Last year	گزشتہ سال	چھُوئی نِیان	Guzista Sal
去世	Qùshì	To pass away	انتقال ہونا	چھُوئی شی	Intiqal hona

Chinese	Pinyin	English	اُردو	چینی تلفظ	Roman Urdu
全	Quán	Whole	سارا	چُھو آن	Sa'raa
缺点	Quēdiǎn	Weakness	کمزوری	چُھوے دیان	Kamzori
却	Què	But	لیکن	چُھوے	Le'keen
确实	Quèshí	Really	حقیقتاً	چُھو شی	Haqi'qatan
群众	Qúnzhòng	Masses	عوام	چھوءن ٹرونگ	Awam
然后	Ránhòu	Afterward	بعد میں	ران ہو	Ba'ad Me
热	Rè	Hot	گرم	رَ	Garm
热爱	Rè'ài	To love deeply	شدید محبت کرنا	رَ آئی	Shadid Mu-habat Karna
热闹	Rènào	Bustling	گہما گہمی	رَناو	Gahma Gahmi
热情	Rèqíng	Warm hearted	خوش اخلاق	رَ چھنگ	Khosh Ikhlaq

Lesson-41

Vocabulary - لغت , Shēngcí，
词汇 Lu'ghut

Chinese	Pinyin	English	اُردو	چینی تلفظ	Roman Urdu
人	Rén	Person	فرد	رِین	Fard
仁慈	Réncí	Kind	مہربان	رِین سی	Meherban
人民	Rénmín	People	عوام	رین مین	Awam
认识	Rènshi	To know	جاننا	رین شی	Ja'anna
认为	Rènwéi	To think	سوچنا	رین وے	Sochna
任务	Rènwù	Task	کام	رین وُ	Ka'am
认真	Rènzhēn	Conscien-tious	ذمہ داری	رین ژین	Zemedari
扔	Rēng	Throw	پھینکنا	رَنگ	Phenkna
日（天）	Rì (tiān)	Day	روز۔ یوم	رِی (تھیان)	Roz/Yom
容易	Róngyì	Easy	آسان	رونگ اِی	Asa'an
肉	Ròu	Meat	گوشت	رو	Gosht
如果	Rúguǒ	If	اگر	روگوآ	Agar
如今	Rújīn	Now	ابھی	روچین	Abhi
弱	Ruò	Weak	کمزور	رُواو	Kamzor

Chinese	Pinyin	English	اُردو	چینی تلفظ	Roman Urdu
三	Sān	Three	تین	سَن	Teen
散步	Sànbù	Walk	پیدل چلنا	سَن پُو	Peydal Chalna
山	Shān	Mountain	پہاڑ	شان	Pa'haar
善良	Shànliáng	Good hearted	خوش دل	شان لیانگ	Khush Dil
伤	Shāng	Wound	زخم	شنگ	Zakham
商店	Shāngdiàn	Shop	دُکان	شنگ تیان	Dukan
商量	Shāngliáng	Discuss	بات چیت	شنگ لیانگ	Ba'at Cheet
上（边）	Shàng (biān)	Up (above)	اوپر	شنگ (پیان)	U'paar
上楼	Shàng lóu	Upstairs	بالائی منزل	شنگ لاو	Bala'i Manzil
上帝	Shàngdì	God	خُدا	شنگ تِی	Khuda
上午	Shàngwǔ	Morning	صبح	شِنگ اُو	Subah
上学	Shàngxué	To go to school	درسی تعلیم	شنگ شوے	Darsee Taleem

Lesson-42

Vocabulary - لغت , Shēngcí，词汇 Lu'ghut

Chinese	Pinyin	English	اُردو	چینی تلفظ	Roman Urdu
上衣	Shàngyī	Coat	کوٹ	شنگ اِی	Coat
少	Shǎo	Little	تھوڑا	شاو	Thora
蛇	Shé	Snake	سانپ	شِ	Sa'anp
设备	Shèbèi	Equip-ment	اوزار	شِ پے	Ao'zaar
社会主义	Shèhuì zhǔyì	Socialism	اشتراکیت	شِ خوئی ٹوئی	Ishtraqiat
深	Shēn	Deep	گہرا	شین	Gahra
身体	Shēntǐ	Health	صحت	شین تھی	Sehat
什么	Shénme	What	کیا	شین ما	Kiya
神仙	Shénxiān	Angel	فرشتہ	شین شیان	Farishta
生产	Shēngchǎn	Output	پیداوار	شنگ ٹھان	Paydawar
生活	Shēnghuó	Life	زندگی	شنگ خو	Zindagi
生命	Shēngmìng	Living	حیات	شنگ مینگ	Heyat
胜利	Shènglì	Victory	فتح	شنگ لِی	Fatah
湿	Shī	Wet	نم	شی	Num

Chinese	Pinyin	English	اُردو	چینی تلفظ	Roman Urdu
时候	Shíhou	Time	وقت	شِ ہو	Waqt
时间	Shíjiān	Time	وقت	شِ چیان	Waqt
食堂	Shítáng	Banquet Hall	طعام خانہ	شِ تھانگ	Tu'am Khana
石头	Shítou	Stone	پتھر	شِ تھو	Pa'thar
是	Shì	Is	ہے	شِ	Hai
世纪	Shìjì	Century	صدی	شِ چِی	Sa'adi
世界	Shìjiè	World	دنیا	شِ چے	Dunya
事情	Shìqíng	Matter	معاملہ	شِ چھنگ	Mamla
收音机	Shōuyīnjī	Radio	ریڈیو	شواینچی	Radio
手	Shǒu	Hand	ہاتھ	شو	Ha'ath
手表	Shǒubiǎo	Watch	دستی گھڑی	شو پیاو	Dasti Ghari
首都	Shǒudū	Capital	دارلحکومت	شو تو	Darul Hu-kumat

Lesson-43

Vocabulary - لغت , Shēngcí，词汇 Lu'ghut

Chinese	Pinyin	English	اُردو	چینی تلفظ	Roman Urdu
手术	Shǒushù	Operation	آپریشن	شَاؤ شو	Operation
首先	Shǒuxiān	Firstly	پہلے	شَاؤ شیان	Pahle
受到	Shòudào	Receive	حاصل کرنا	شَاؤ تاو	Hasil Karna
售货员	Shòuhuòyuán	Salesman	سیلز مین	شو خو یو آن	Salesman
受压迫	Shòu yāpò	Oppressed	مظلوم	شو یا پھو	Mazloom
书	Shū	Book	کتاب	شُو	Kitab
书店	Shūdiàn	Bookstore	کتاب کی دُکان	شو تیان	Kitab ki Du'kan
舒服	Shūfú	Comfort-able	آرام دہ	شُو فو	Ara'am dah
叔叔	Shūshu	Uncle	چچا	شُو شو	Chacha
树	Shù	Tree	درخت	شُو	Darkht
树叶	Shùyè	Leaves	پتے	شُوے	Pat'te
谁	Shuí	Who	کون	شوئی	Ko'n
水	Shuǐ	Water	پانی	شُوئی	Paani
水果	Shuǐguǒ	Fruit	پھل	شوئی گو آ	Phal

Chinese	Pinyin	English	اُردو	چینی تلفظ	Roman Urdu
水库	Shuǐkù	Reservoir	آبی ذخیرہ	شوئی کھو	A'abi Zakh-ira
水灾	Shuǐzāi	Flood disaster	سیلابی تباہی	شُوئی ذائی	Selabi Tabahi
睡	Shuì	Sleep	نیند سونا	شوئی	Neend Sona
说	Shuō	To speak	بولنا	شُواو	Bol'na
说明	Shuōmíng	Explain	سمجھانا	شواومِنگ	Sam'jhana
思想	Sīxiǎng	Ideology	فلسفہ	سی شیانگ	Falsafa
死（了）	Sǐ (le)	To die	انتقال ہونا	سِی (لا)	Intiqal Hona
四	Sì	Four	چار	سی	Char
送	Sòng	To send	بھیجنا	سونگ	Bhejna
苏醒	Sūxǐng	Revive	بیدار کرنا	سُو شِنگ	Be'daar Karna
虽然	Suīrán	Although	اگرچہ	سوئی ران	Agarche
岁	Suì	Age	عمر	سُوئی	Umar

Lesson-44

Vocabulary - لغت , Shēngcí ,
词汇 Lu’ghut

Chinese	Pinyin	English	اُردو	چینی تلفظ	Roman Urdu
他/她/它	Tā/tā/tā	He/She/It	وہ (یہ)	تھا	Woh
他们	Tāmen	They	وہ لوگ	تھامین	Woh’log
太	Tài	Very	بہت	تھاے	Bahut
太	Tài	Too	بھی	تھاے	Bhi
太阳	Tàiyáng	Sun	سورج	تھایانگ	Suraj
探亲	Tànqīn	Visit family	خاندان ملن	تھان چھِن	Khandan Milan
汤	Tāng	Soup	سوپ	تھانگ	Soup
糖	Táng	Sweet	میٹھا	تھانگ	Meetha
躺	Tǎng	To lie down	لیٹنا	تھاآنگ	Le’tna
讨论	Tǎolùn	To discuss	مذاکرہ	تھاولُوءن	Muzakra
特别	Tèbié	Particu-larly	خاصکر	تھہ پیے	Khaskar
疼	Téng	Pain	درد	تھنگ	Dard
提包	Tíbāo	Satchel	تھیلا/بیگ	تھی پاو	Baag/ Thaila
提高	Tígāo	To raise	بلند کرنا	تھی کاو	Buland Karna

Chinese	Pinyin	English	اُردو	چینی تلفظ	Roman Urdu
体温	Tǐwēn	Body temperature	جسمانی حرارت	تھی وین	Jismani Hararat
体育	Tǐyù	Sports	اسپورٹس	تھی وی	Sports
体育馆	Tǐyùguǎn	Sports stadium	اسپورٹس اسٹیڈیم	تھی ویگو آن	Sports stadium
天	Tiān	Sky	آسمان	تھیان	Asma'an
天气	Tiānqì	Weather	موسم	تِھیان چھی	Mau'sim
铁	Tiě	Iron	لوہا	تھی اِے	Lo'ha
听	Tīng	Listen	سُننا	تھینگ	Sun'na
听说	Tīng shuō	Hearsay	افواہ	تِھنگ شوو	Afwah
同意	Tóngyì	Agree	قبول کرنا	تھونگ اِی	Qabul Karna
同志	Tóngzhì	Comrade	کامریڈ	تھونگ ژِ	Comrade

Lesson-45

Vocabulary - لغت , Shēngcí，词汇 Lu'ghut

Chinese	Pinyin	English	اُردو	چینی تلفظ	Roman Urdu
头	Tóu	Head	سر	تھو	Saar
图书馆	Túshū guǎn	Library	لاءبریری	تھو شو کو آن	Library
土地	Tǔdì	Land	زمین	تھوتِی	Zameen
团结	Tuánjié	Unity	اتحاد	تھوآن جیے	Ittehad
腿	Tuǐ	Leg	پیر	تھوی	Pa'er
挖	Wā	To dig	کھودنا	وآ	Khodna
袜子	Wàzi	Socks	موزہ	وآذہ	Moza
外边	Wàibian	Outside	باہر طرف	وآئی پیان	Bahar Tarf
外国	Wàiguó	Foreign	غیر ملک	وآئی ۔ کو آ	Gair Mulk
外国人	Wàiguó rén	Foreigner	غیر ملکی	وآئی۔ کو آ۔ رین	Gair Mulki
完（了）	Wán (le)	Finish	ختم ہو گیا	وآن (لہ)	Khatam-Ho'gaya
完成	Wánchéng	To com-plete	مکمل کرنا	وآن چھنگ	Mukamal Karna
完全	Wánquán	All/total	مکمل / سارا	وآن چھو آن	Sara/ Mu-kamal
玩	Wán	To play	کھیلنا	وآنر	Khelna

Chinese	Pinyin	English	اُردو	چینی تلفظ	Roman Urdu
完整	Wánzhěng	Intact	صحیح سالم	وآن ژنگ	Sahee Salem
碗	Wǎn	Bowl	پیالہ	وآن	Piyala
晚	Wǎn	Late	دیر	وآن	D'er
晚饭	Wǎnfàn	Supper	رات کا کھانا	وآن فان	Ra'at Ka Khana
晚会	Wǎnhuì	Evening party	رات کی ضیافت	وآن خوئی	Ra'at ki Ziyafat
晚上	Wǎnshàng	Evening	شام	وآن شنگ	Sha'am
万	Wàn	Ten thou-sand	دس ہزار	وآن	Das Hazar
万岁	Wànsuì	Long live	زندہ باد	وآن سوئی	Zindabad
忘（了）	Wàng (le)	To forget	بھول جانا	وانگ لہ	Bhul jana
危险	Wéixiǎn	Danger	خطرہ	ویشیان	Kha'tra
伟大	Wěidà	Great	عظیم	وے تا	Azeem

Lesson-46

Vocabulary - لغت , Shēngcí ، 词汇 Lu'ghut

Chinese	Pinyin	English	اُردو	چینی تلفظ	Roman Urdu
慰劳	Wèilào	To appre-ciate	تعریف کرنا	وِیلا و	Tareef Karna
为了	Wèile	For	کے لیے	وِیلہ	Ke Liye
为设么	Wèi shè me	Why	کیوں	وِے شینما	Kion
文化	Wénhuà	Culture	ثقافت	وین خوا	Saqafat
文化大革命	Wénhuà dàgémìng	Cultural Revolu-tion	ثقافتی انقلاب	وِینخواتا کمینگ	Sakafati Inqilab
文物	Wénwù	Cultural relics	ثقافتی نوادرات	وین وُ	Sakafati-Nawadrat
文学	Wénxué	Literature	ادب	وین شُوے	Adaab
文章	Wénzhāng	Article	مضمون	وین چانگ	Mazmun
问	Wèn	To ask	پوچھنا	وِین	Puuchna
问题	Wèntí	Question	سوال	وِین ٹھی	Sawal
我	Wǒ	I	میں	و	Ma'n
我们	Wǒmen	We	ہم	ومین	Hum
握手	Wòshǒu	Shake hands	ہاتھ ملانا	وشاو	Ha'athMi-lana
舞蹈	Wǔdǎo	Dance	رقص	اُوتاو	Rakhsh

Chinese	Pinyin	English	اُردو	چینی تلفظ	Roman Urdu
午饭	Wǔfàn	Lunch	دوپہر کا کھانا	وُفان	Dopahar Ka Khana
西	Xi	West	مغرب	شی	Maghrib
喜欢	Xǐhuan	To like	پسند کرنا	شی خوآن	Pasand Karna
洗澡	Xǐzǎo	Take bath	نہانا	شی ذاو	Nahana
下边	Xiàbian	Down below	نیچے	شِیاپیان	Neeche
夏天	Xiàtiān	Summer	گرمی	شِیاتھیان	Garmee
下午	Xiàwǔ	Afternoon	سہ پہر	شِیاو	Sehpahar
下雨	Xià yǔ	To rain	بارش ہونا	شِیاایوی	Ba'rish Hona
先	Xiān	First	اول	شِیان	Awa'al
先进	Xiānjìn	Advanced	جدید	شِیان چِن	Jadeed
先生	Xiānshēng	Mr/ Gentleman	صاحب/جناب	شِیان شَنگ	Janab/Saheb
献(血)	Xiàn (xuè)	Donate blood	خون کا عطیہ	شِیان شیے	Khoon kaAttya
现在	Xiànzài	Now	ابھی	شِیان زاے	Abhi
相当	Xiāngdāng	Equivalent	برابر	شِیانگ تانگ	Barabar

Lesson-47

Vocabulary - لغت , Shēngcí ,
词汇 Lu'ghut

Chinese	Pinyin	English	اُردو	چینی تلفظ	Roman Urdu
相信	Xiāngxìn	Believe	یقین	شیانگ شِن	Yaqeen
香烟	Xiāngyān	Cigarette	سگریٹ	شیانگ یان	Cigarette
箱子	Xiāngzi	Trunk	صندوق	شیانگ زہ	Sandooq
想	Xiǎng	To want	چاہنا	شیانگ	Cha'hna
享受	Xiǎngshòu	To enjoy	مزے کرنا	شیانگ شو	Maze Karna
向	Xiàng	Towards	طرف	شیانگ	Tarf
项目	Xiàngmù	Item	آیٹم	شیانگ مُو	Item
消灭	Xiāomiè	To wipe out	نیست و نابود کرنا	شیاو میے	Nest Na-bood Karna
小	Xiǎo	Small	چھوٹا	شیاو	Chota
小孩	Xiǎohái	Child	بچہ	شیاو ہر	Ba'chha
小卖部	Xiǎomàibù	Shop	شاپ/دُکان	شیاو مائی پُو	Dukan
小时	Xiǎoshí	Hour	گھنٹہ	شیاو شی	Ghanta
小学	Xiǎoxué	Primary school	پرائمری سکول	شیاو شُوے	Primary school
笑	Xiào	To laugh	ہنسنا	شیاو	Hansna

Chinese	Pinyin	English	اُردو	چینی تلفظ	Roman Urdu
鞋	Xié	Shoes	جوتا	شیے	Joo'ta
谢谢	Xièxiè	Thank	شُکریہ	شیے شیے	Shukr'ya
心	Xīn	Heart	دل	شِین	Dil
新闻	Xīnwén	News	خبر	شین وین	Khabar
兴奋	Xīngfèn	Exciting	پُر مسرت	شینگ فین	Pur Mussarat
行动	Xíngdòng	Action	عمل	شینگ تونگ	Ama'al
醒	Xǐng	Wake up	جاگنا	شینگ	Ja'gna
幸福	Xìngfú	Happiness	خوشی	شِنگ فو	Khu'shi
修理	Xiūlǐ	Repair	مرمت	شِیولی	Mara'mat
休息	Xiūxí	To rest	آرام کرنا	شیو شی	Ara'am Karna
修正	Xiūzhèng	To restore	ٹھیک کرنا	شیو ڑنگ	Theek Karna
虚心	Xūxīn	Modest	انکسار/عاجز	شوئَ شین	A'ajeez/ Inkisar
需要	Xūyào	To need	طلب / ضرورت	شوئَ یاو	Zarurat/ Talab
许多	Xǔduō	Many	زیادہ/بہت	شوئَ ٹُوو	Bahut/Ziya-dah

Lesson-48

Vocabulary - لغت , Shēngcí ，词汇 Lu'ghut

Chinese	Pinyin	English	اُردو	چینی تلفظ	Roman Urdu
学生	Xuéshēng	Student	طالب علم	شُوے شنگ	Talib Ilm
学习	Xuéxí	Study	پڑھنا	شوے شی	Parhna
学校	Xuéxiào	School	اسکول	شوے شیاو	School
雪	Xuě	Snow	برف	شوے	Barf
雪白	Xuěbái	Snow white	برفانی سفید	شُوے پائی	Barfani Sufaid
压迫	Yāpò	To oppress	ظلم کرنا	یاپھو	Zulm Karna
言	Yán	Inundated	زیر آب	یان	Zere-Ab
严格	Yángé	Strict	سخت	یان گہ	Sakht
研究	Yánjiū	To study	تحقیق کرنا	یان چِیو	Tahqeeq Karna
眼睛	Yǎnjīng	Eye	آنکھ / چشم	یان چِنگ	Chasham/ Ankh
样	Yàng	Kind	مہربان	یانگ	Meherban
要求	Yāoqiú	Demand	طلب / مطالبہ	یاو چھِیو	Mutalba/ Talab
咬	Yǎo	Bite	کاٹنا	یاو	Ka'tna
要	Yào	Want	چاہنا	یاو	Chah'na

Chinese	Pinyin	English	اُردو	چینی تلفظ	Roman Urdu
也	Yě	Also	بھی	یہ	Bhi
也许	Yěxǔ	Perhaps	شاءد	یہ شوئی	Sha'ed
夜	Yè	Night	رات	یہ	Ra'at
衣服	Yīfú	Clothes	کپڑا	اِی فو	Kapr'ra
医疗	Yīliáo	Medical treatment	علاج معالجہ	اِی لیاو	Ilaaj-mualja
医疗品	Yīliáo pǐn	Medicines	دوا	اِی لیاو پھین	Da'waa
医生	Yīshēng	Doctor	ڈاکٹر	اِی شنگ	Doctor
一定	Yīdìng	Certainly	یقینی	اِی دینگ	Yaqeeni
一共	Yīgòng	All togeth-er	سب ملا کر	اِی کونگ	Sab Mila Kar
一样	Yīyàng	Same	ایک طرح	اِی یانگ	Ek Tarah
以后	Yǐhòu	After	بعد	اِی ہو	Ba'ad
已经	Yǐjīng	Already	قبل	اِی چنگ	Qa'bal

Lesson-49

Vocabulary - لغت , Shēngcí，词汇 Lu'ghut

Chinese	Pinyin	English	اُردو	چینی تلفظ	Roman Urdu
以前	Yǐqián	Ago	پہلے	اِی چھِیان	Pahle
以为	Yǐwéi	To think	سوچنا	اِی وَے	Sochna
椅子	Yǐzi	Chair	کرسی	اِی زہ	Kur'see
以便	Yǐbiàn	Same time	ساتھ ہی ساتھ	اِی پیان (اِی پیان)	Sath-hi-Sath
一会儿	Yīhuǐ'er	A moment	ایک لمحہ	اِی خوار	Ek lamha
意见	Yìjiàn	Opinion	رائے	اِی چیان	Rai
议论	Yìlùn	To discuss	بحث کرنا	اِی لوءن	Bahas Karna
一起	Yīqǐ	Together	ایک ساتھ	اِی چھی	Ek Saath
艺术	Yìshù	Art work	فن تخلیق / کاریگری	اِی شو (پین)	Fun/Karig-ari Takh-leeq
意思	Yìsi	Meaning	معنیٰ	اِی سی	Ma'ani
意义	Yìyì	Effect	اثر	اِی اِی	A'sar
阴	Yīn	Cloudy	بادل	اِین	Badal
因为	Yīnwèi	Because	کیونکہ	اِین وے	Ku'nke
音乐	Yīnyuè	Music	موسیقی	اِین یُوے	Mo'seqi

Chinese	Pinyin	English	اُردو	چینی تلفظ	Roman Urdu
影响	Yǐngxiǎng	Impression	تاثیر	اِین شِیانگ	Ta'seer
应该	Yīnggāi	Should	ضرور	اِین گاے	Zaroor
英雄	Yīngxióng	Hero	عظیم شخصیت	اِینگ شِیونگ	Azeem Shakh'siat
迎（欢）	Yíng (huan)	Welcome	استقبال کرنا	اِینگ (خوان)	Istiqbal Karna
用	Yòng	Use	استعمال کرنا	یونگ	Istema'al Karna
邮局	Yóujú	Post office	پوسٹ آفس	یُو چُوئی	Post office
游览	Yóulǎn	Sightseeing	سیر تفریح	یو لان	Sa'ar Ta-freeh
邮票	Yóupiào	Stamp	ڈاک ٹکٹ	یُوپھِیاو	Dak Ticket
游泳	Yóuyǒng	Swim	تیرنا	یو یونگ	Tair'na
有	Yǒu	Has/Have	پاس ہونا	یو	Pass Hona
有的	Yǒu de	Some	کچھ	یودا	Kuu'ch
友好	Yǒuhǎo	Friendly	دوستی	یو خاو	Dosti

Lesson-50

Vocabulary - لغت , Shēngcí , 词汇 Lu'ghut

Chinese	Pinyin	English	اُردو	چینی تلفظ	Roman Urdu
又名	Yòu míng	Famous	مشہور	یو مینگ	Mash'hur
友谊	Yǒuyì	Friend-ship	دوستی	یو اِی	Dosti
右	Yòu	Right	دایاں / سیدھا	یُو	Daya'an-Seedha
又	Yòu	Again	دوبارہ / پھر	یُو	Phir Do-bara
鱼	Yú	Fish	مچھلی	اِیوی	Machli
雨	Yǔ	Rain	بارش	اِیوی	Ba'rish
羽毛球	Yǔmáoqiú	Badmin-ton	بیڈمنٹن	اِیوماو چھیو	Badminton
原来	Yuánlái	Origi-nally	اصل میں	یُوآن لاے	Asal me
原谅	Yuánliàng	Excuse/ Forgive	معاف کرنا	یُوآن لِیانگ	Mu'af Karna
原料	Yuánliào	Raw ma-terial	خام مال	یُوآن لیاو	Khaam Mal
远	Yuǎn	Distant	دور	یُوآن	Dor
原则	Yuánzé	Principle	اصول	یُوآن ذہ	U'sool
月	Yuè	Month	مہینہ	یُواِے	Ma'hina
越来越（多）	Yuè lái yuè (duō)	The more	زیادہ سے زیادہ	یُوے لاے یُوے (توو)	Ziyadah se ziyadah

Chinese	Pinyin	English	اُردو	چینی تلفظ	Roman Urdu
运动	Yùndòng	Sports	اسپورٹس	ایون تونگ	Sports
运动员	Yùndòngyuán	Sports-man	اسپورٹس مین	ایون تونگ یوآن	Sportsman
运走	Yùn zǒu	Carry away	لے جانا	ایون ذاو	Le- jana
杂志	Zázhì	Maga-zine	رسالہ	ذاژِ	Re'sala
在	Zài	Inside	اندر	ذاے	Under
再	Zài	Again	پھر	ذاے	Phir
再见	Zàijiàn	Good bye	الوداع	ذاے چیان	Al'weeda
咱们	Zánmen	We	ہم لوگ	ذان مین	Hum log
赞成	Zànchéng	Approve	قبول کرنا	ذان ٹھنگ	Qabul karna
早	Zǎo	Early	قبل از وقت	ذاو	Qabal -az Waqt

Lesson-51

Vocabulary - لغت , Shēngcí ' 词汇 Lu'ghut

Chinese	Pinyin	English	اُردو	چینی تلفظ	Roman Urdu
早饭	Zǎofàn	Breakfast	ناشتہ	ذاو فن	Na'shta
早上	Zǎoshang	Morning	صبح	ذاوشنگ	Subah
造	Zào	To build	بنانا	ذاو	Banana
怎么	Zěnme	How	کیسے	ذین ما	Kaise
怎么样	Zěnme yàng	How are you?	آپ کا کیا حال ہے	ذین ما یانگ	KiyaHa'al Hai
崭新	Zhǎnxīn	Brand new	بالکل نیا	ژان شین	Bilqul Naya
站	Zhàn	To stand	کھڑا ہونا	ژان	Kharra Hona
战士	Zhànshì	Soldier	سپاہی	ژان شی	Si'pahi
战争	Zhànzhēng	War	جنگ	ژان ژنگ	Ja'ng
张开	Zhāng kāi	To open	کھولنا	ژان کھائے	Kho'lna
招待	Zhāodài	To receive	میزبانی کرنا	ژاوتاے	Mezbani Karna
招待会	Zhāodài huì	Reception	ضیافت	ژاوتاءخوئی	Ziyafat
找	Zhǎo	To look for	ڈھونڈنا	ژاو	Dhund'na
照相	Zhàoxiàng	To take pictures	تصویر لینا	ژاو شیانگ	Tasweer Lena

Chinese	Pinyin	English	اُردو	چینی تلفظ	Roman Urdu
照相机	Zhàoxiàngjī	Camera	کیمرہ	ژاو شیانگ چی	Camera
这个	Zhège	This	یہ	ژیگا	Yeh
这里	Zhèlǐ	Here	یہاں	ژیرلی	Yi'haan
真（的）	Zhēn (de)	Really	حقیقتاً	ژین(دا)	Haqeetan Such me
这样	Zhèyàng	Like this	اِس طرح	ژ یانگ	Is tarah
政府	Zhèngfǔ	Govern-ment	حکومت	ژنگ فو	Hukumat
政治	Zhèngzhì	Politics	سیاست	ژنگ ژِ	Si'yasat
之一	Zhī yī	Amongst	درمیان میں	ژِ اِی	Darmiyan me
知道	Zhīdào	To know	معلوم ہونا	ژِ تاو	Ma'alum Hona
纸	Zhǐ	Paper	کاغذ	ژِ	Ka'gaz
指	Zhǐ	Point out	اشارہ کرنا	ژِ	Ishara Karna

Lesson-52

Vocabulary - لغت , Shēngcí， 词汇 Lu'ghut

Chinese	Pinyin	English	اُردو	چینی تلفظ	Roman Urdu
只	Zhǐ	Only	صرف	ژ	Si'rf
智慧	Zhìhuì	Intelligent	ذہانت	ژ خوئی	Zahanat
质量	Zhìliàng	Quality	کیفیت / قسم	ژلیانگ	Qism/ Me'yar
致命	Zhìmìng	Fatal	مُہلک	ژِمینگ	Muhliq
制造	Zhìzào	Manufac-tured	بنا ہوا	ژِ ذاؤ	Bana Hu'a
中国制造	Zhōngguó zhìzào	Made in China	چین کا بنا ہوا	چونگو آژذاؤ	Cheen ka bana hu'a
中华	Zhōnghuá	Chinese	چینی	چونگ خوآ	Cheeni
中文	Zhōngwén	Chinese language	چینی زبان	چونگ وین	Cheeni Zaban
中学	Zhōngxué	Middle school	مِڈل اسکول	چونگ شوے	Middle school
终于	Zhōngyú	Finally	آخرکار	چونگ اِیوی	A'akheer ka'r
种	Zhǒng	Type	قسم	چُونگ	Qism
重要	Zhòngyào	Important	اہم	چُونگ یاو	Aha'am
祝	Zhù	To wish	خواہش	چُو	Khua'hish
祝贺	Zhùhè	To con-gratulate	مبارک دینا	چُوخہ	Mubarak Dena

Chinese	Pinyin	English	اُردو	چینی تلفظ	Roman Urdu
住宅	Zhùzhái	House	عمارت	چُوچاے	E'marat
装	Zhuāng	To contain	قابو کرنا	چُوآنگ	Qabu Karna
壮丽	Zhuànglì	To assem-ble	جمع کرنا	چوآنگ لِی	Jama'a Karna
准许	Zhǔnxǔ	To allow	اجازت دینا	ٹوءن شوئی	Ijazat dena
捉住	Zhuō zhù	To catch	پکڑنا	ٹواوچُو	Pakar'na
桌子	Zhuōzi	Table	میز	ٹو آذہ	Me'ez
子	Zi	Word	لفظ	ذی	La'fz
自己	Zìjǐ	Self	خود	ذی چی	Khud
只	Zhǐ	Only	صرف	ٹرِ	Sirf

Lesson-53

Vocabulary - لغت , Shēngcí ، 词汇 Lu'ghut

Chinese	Pinyin	English	اُردو	چینی تلفظ	Roman Urdu
自力更生	Zìlìgēng-shēng	Self reliant	خود انحصاری	ذی لی کنگ شنگ	Khud-Inhasari
自行车	Zìxíngchē	Bicycle	سائیکل	ذی شِنگ چھ	Cycle
自由	Zìyóu	Freedom	آزادی	ذی یاو	Azadi
走	Zǒu	Walk	چلنا	ذو	Chalna
祖国	Zǔguó	Mother-land	مادر وطن	ذوکوآ	Madr-i Watan
嘴	Zuǐ	Mouth	منہ	ذوئی	Munh
最	Zuì	Most	بہت	ذُوئی	Bahut
最好	Zuì hǎo	Best	سب سے اچھا	ذُوئی خاو	Sab-se Ach'cha
最后	Zuìhòu	Finally	آخرکار	ذُوئی ہو	Akhir Kar
最近	Zuìjìn	Recently	حال میں	ذوی چن	Haal -me
昨天	Zuótiān	Yesterday	گزشتہ کل	ذو تھیان	Guzishta Kal
左	Zuǒ	Left	بایاں	ذُو	Bayaan
坐	Zuò	Sit down	بیٹھنا	ذُو	Bai'thna
做	Zuò	To do	کرنا	ذُو	Ka'rna
作为	Zuòwéi	As it is	جیسا بھی	ذُوِوے	Jaisa bhi

Lesson-54

Common Words – عام استعمال کے الفاظ , Pǔtōng cí，普通词Aam Alfaz

Chinese	Pinyin	English	اُردو	چینی تلفظ	Roman Urdu
好	Hǎo	Good/ok	اچھا/ ٹھیک	خاؤ	Acha/Thik
坏	Huài	Bad/wick-ed	خراب / بُرا	خو آئی	Kharab/ Bura
对	Duì	All right	ٹھیک / صحیح	تو ئی	Theek/Sa-hee
无	Wú	No	نہیں	وو	Nahee
快	Kuài	Fast	جلد	کھوائی	Jald
慢	Màn	Slow	آہستہ	مَن	Ahista
现在	Xiànzài	Now	ابھی / حال	شیان زائے	Abhi
以后	Yǐhòu	After	بعد میں	اِی ہو	Baad Me
早	Zǎo	Early	جلدی	ذآؤ	Jaldi
晚	wǎn	Late	دیر	وآن	Der
太	Tài	Too	زیادہ	تھائی	Ziyada
很	Hěn	Very	زیادہ	خین	Bahut
很好	Hěn hǎo	Too good	بہت اچھا	خین ہاؤ	Bahut Acha

Chinese	Pinyin	English	اُردو	چینی تلفظ	Roman Urdu
漂亮	Piàoliang	Beautiful	خوش شکل	پھیاؤ لیانگ	Khub-soorat
美丽	Měilì	Pretty	حسین (جگہ)	مے لی	Haseen
也	Yě	Also (too)	بھی	یے	Bhi
新	Xīn	New	نیا	شِین	Naya
旧	Jiù	Old	پُرانا	چِی یو	Purana
老	Lǎo	Old	پُرانا	لاؤ	Zaeef
老朋友	Lǎo péngyǒu	Old friend	پُرانا دوست	لاؤ پھانگیو	Purana Dost
再	Zài	Again	پھر / دوبارہ	ذآئی	Dobarah

Lesson-55

Common Words – عام استعمال کے الفاظ , Pŭtōng cí，普通词Am Alfaz

Chinese	Pinyin	English	اُردو	چینی تلفظ	Roman Urdu
白	Bái	White	سفید	پائے	Sufaid
黑	Hēi	Black	کالا	خے اِی	Kala
难	Nán	Difficult	مشکل	نان	Mushkil
容易	Róngyì	Easy	آسان	رونگ اِی	Asan
忙	Máng	Busy	مصروف	مانگ	Masroof
没事	Méishì	No work	بے کار	مے شی	Baykaar
什么	Shénme	What	کیا	شیں ما	Kiya
怎么样	Zé me yàng	How	کیسے / کیسا	زِمین یانگ	Kaise/Kaisa
谁	Shuí	Who	کون	شوئی	Kon
这	Zhè	This	یہ	چی	Yeh
这个	Zhège	This one	یہ والا	چیگا	Yeh Wala
哪个	Năge	Which one	کونسا	ناگا	Konsa
那个	Nàgè	That one	وہ والا	نے گا	Who wala

Chinese	Pinyin	English	اُردو	چینی تلفظ	Roman Urdu
这儿	Zhè'er	Here	یہاں	چیار	Yihaan
那儿	Nà'er	There	وہاں	نار	Wahaan
是	Shì	Is	ہے	شِی	Hai
的	De	Of	کا	دا	Ka
他的	Tā de	His	اس کا	تھا دا	Uska
你的	Nǐ de	Yours	تمہارا	نِی دا	Tumhara
可以	Kěyǐ	Ok, yes	ہاں	کھ ای	Haan
请	Qǐng	Please	مہربانی کریں	چھینگ	Mehrban Karen i
别	Bié	Do not	منع کرنا	پِی اے	Mana Kar-nazxc
别走	Bié zǒu	Do not go	مت جاؤ	پِی اے زاؤ	Mut Jao

Lesson-56

Colours - رنگ - یانسا , Yánsè ,
颜色 Rung

Chinese	Pinyin	English	اُردو	چینی تلفظ	Roman Urdu
红	Hóng	Red	لال / سرخ	خونگ	Lal/Surkh
红色	Hóngsè	Red colour	سرخ / لال رنگ	خونگ سا	Surkh/Lal Rang
白	Bái	White	سفید رنگ	پائے	Sufaid Rang
黑	Hēi	Black	کالارنگ	ہے اِی	Kala Rang
绿	Lǜ	Green	سبز رنگ	لوئی	Sabz Rang
蓝	Lán	Blue	نیلہ / آسمانی	لا آن	Neela/As-mani
棕	Zōng	Brown	بھورا / چاکلیٹ رنگ	زونگ	Bhura/ Chocolate Rang
黄	Huáng	Yellow	پیلا / زرد	خُوآنگ	Peela/Zard
浅/淡	Qīng	Light	ہلکا رنگ	چھنگ	Halka Rang
深	Shēn	Deep	بھاری / گہرہ رنگ	شین	Gahra/ Bhari Rang

Add 'se' with the word to get desired meaning.
Example: Hongse (لال والا)
Shense (گہرا والا)

Lesson-57

Common words - عام الفاظ , Pǔtōng cí，普通词 Aam Alfaz

Chinese	Pinyin	English	اُردو	چینی تلفظ	Roman Urdu
世界	Shìjiè	World	دنیا	شی چے	Dunya
数字	Shùzi	Number	عدد	شُوزہ	Adad
平方	Píngfāng	Square	مربع	پھینگ فانگ	Murabba
下雨	Xià yǔ	Raining	بارش	شیا اِیوی	Bareesh
下雪	Xià xuě	Snowfall	برفباری	شیا شُوے	Barf Bari
刮风	Guā fēng	Windy	طوفان	کو آفنگ	Toofan
暖和	Nuǎnhuo	Warm	گرم	نو آن خو	Garm
凉快	Liàng kuài	Pleasant	خوشگوار	لیانگ کھوائی	Khushga-war
冷	Lěng	Cold	سرد	لانگ	Sard
热	Rè	Hot	گرم	ر	Garm
沙漠	Shāmò	Desert	ریگستان	شامُو	Registan
左边	Zuǒ biàn	Left	بائیں طرف	ذوپین	Bayen tarf
右边	Yòu biàn	Right	دائیں طرف	یو پین	Dayen tarf

Chinese	Pinyin	English	اُردو	چینی تلفظ	Roman Urdu
质量	Zhìliàng	Quality	معیار	ژِلیانگ	Meyar
高	Gāo	High	اونچا	کاؤ	Uuncha
差	Chà	Poor (bad)	خراب	ٹھا	Kharab
平方	Píngfāng	Area	رقبہ	پھنگ فانگ	Raqba
英里	Yīnglǐ	Mile	میل	اِینگ لی	meel
能源	Néngyuán	Energy	توانائی	ننگ یُو آن	Tawanai
刮风	Guā fēng	Wind	ہوا	کوافنگ	Hawa
阴	Yīn	Cloud	بادل	اِیون	Badal
光年	Guāng nián	Light year	نوری سال	گوانگ نیان	Noori Saal

Lesson-58

Common words - عام الفاظ , Pǔtōng cí，普通词Aam Alfaz

Chinese	Pinyin	English	اُردو	چینی تلفظ	Roman Urdu
商场	Shāngc-hǎng	Super Market	سپر مارکیٹ	شنگ ٹھانگ	Super Market
小卖铺	Xiǎo mài Bù	Shop	دکان	شیاؤمائی پُو	Dookan
路	Lù	Street	سڑک	لُو	Sarak
街	Jiē	Road	شاہراہ	جیئے	Shahra-e
对面	Duìmiàn	Opposite	آمنے سامنے	توئی میانز	Amne-Samne
前边	Qiánbian	Infront	سامنے	چھیان پیانز	Samne
后边	Hòubian	Backside	پیچھے	خو پیانز	Peeche
朋友	Péngyǒu	Friend	دوست	پھانگ یو	Dost
敌人	Dírén	Enemy	دُشمن	تِی رین	Dushman
好人	Hǎorén	Gentleman	شریف آدمی	خاؤ رین	Sharif Admi
坏人	Huàirén	Wicked person	خراب آدمی	خوآئی رین	Kharab Admi

Chinese	Pinyin	English	اُردو	چینی تلفظ	Roman Urdu
河	Hé	River	دریا	خا	Darya
海	Hăi	Sea	سمندر	ہائے	Samundar
山	Shān	Mountain	پہاڑ	شان	Pahar
农村	Nóng chún	Village	گاؤں	نونگ سوءن	Gaon
城市	Chéngshì	City/town	شہر	ٹھنگ شی	Shahar
首都	Shŏudū	Capital	دارلخلافہ	شوتُو	Darulkhi-lafa
政府	Zhèngfŭ	Govern-ment	حکومت	ژنگ فو	Hukumat
中心	Zhōngxīn	Centre	مرکز	چونگ شن	Markaz
商业	Shāngyè	Commerce	تجارت	شنگیے	Teejarat
省	Shěng	Province	صوبہ	شانگ	Sooba
自治区	Zìzhŭ	Autono-mous	خود مختار علاقہ	ذیتی چھوئی	Khud-mukhtar Ilaqa
市长	Shì zhăng	Mayor	ناظم	شی ژانگ	Nazim

Lesson-59

Common words - عام الفاظ , Pǔtōng cí , 普通词 Aam Alfaz

Chinese	Pinyin	English	اُردو	چینی تلفظ	Roman Urdu
中央	Zhōngyāng	Central	مرکزی	چونگ یانگ	Markazi
省政府	Shěng zhèngfǔ	Provincial govt.	صوبائی حکومت	شنگ ژنگفو	Soobai Hukumat
市政府	Shì zhèngfǔ	City government	شہری حکومت	شی ژنگفو	Shahri Hukumat
省长	Shěng zhǎng	Province governor	صوبائی گورنر	شنگ ژانگ	Soobai Governor
党	Dǎng	Party	پارٹی	تانگ	Party
共产党	Gòngchǎndǎng	Communist Party	کمیونسٹ پارٹی	گونگچان تانگ	Communist Party
堂的主席	Dǎng zhǔxí	Party chairman	پارٹی چیرمین	تانگ چُوسی	Party chairman
堂书记	Dǎng shūjì	Party secretary	پارٹی سیکریٹری	تانگ شوچی	Party secretary
公务员	Gōngwùyuán	Civil Servant	سرکاری افسر	کونگو یوآن	Sarkari Afsar
官	Guān	Government official	سرکاری افسر	کو آنر	Sarkari Afsar
大官	Dà guān	High official	اعلیٰ افسر	تا کو انر	Ala Afsar
县官/县长	Xiàn guānyuán	County official	ڈسٹرکٹ افسر	شیان کوانر	District Officer

Chinese	Pinyin	English	اُردو	چینی تلفظ	Roman Urdu
警察	Jǐngchá	Police	پولیس	چنگ ٹھا	Police
法	Fǎ	Law	قانون	فالُوی	Qanoon
检查	Jiǎnchá	Investi-gate	تحقیقات کرنا	چیان ٹھا	Tahqiqat Karna
考察	Kǎochá	Examine	غور کرنا	کھاؤ ٹھا	Ghor Karna
破坏	Pō huái	Disturb	خلل ڈالنا	پھو خوآئی	Khalal Dalna
和平	Hépíng	Peace	امن	خا پھِنگ	Aman
安定	Āndìng	Harmony	سکون	آن تِنگ	Sakoon
团结	Tuánjié	Unite	اتحاد	تھوآن چیے	Ittehad
保护	Bǎohù	Safeguard	حفاظت کرنا	پاؤ خو	Hifazat Karna

Lesson-60

Common Words – عام الفاظ , Pǔtōng cí，普通词Aam Alfaz

Chinese	Pinyin	English	اُردو	چینی تلفظ	Roman Urdu
忙	Máng	Busy	مصروف	مانگ	Masroof
累	Lèi	Tired	تھکا ہوا	لے (لا)	Thaka Hua
難	Nán	Difficult	مشکل	نان	Mushkil
容易	Róngyì	Easy	آسان	رونگ اِی	Asan
貴	Guì	Expensive	مہنگا	گُوئی	Mahnga
便宜	Piányi	Cheap	سستا	پھیان اِی	Susta
懂了	Dǒngle	Understand	سمجھنا	دونگ (لا)	Samghna
謝謝	Xièxiè	Thank you	شکریا (آپکا)	شیئے شیئے	Shukriya
再見	Zàijiàn	See you again	پھر ملاقات ہو گی	ذآئی چیان	Phir Mu-lakat hogi
再會	Zài huì	See you	اگلی ملاقات تک	ذآئی خوئی	Agli Mu-lakat tak

Chinese	Pinyin	English	اُردو	چینی تلفظ	Roman Urdu
多謝	Duōxiè	Many thanks	بہت شکریہ	تُواو شیئے	Bahut Shukriya
太感謝	Tài gǎnxiè	Lots of thanks	بے حد شکریہ	تھائی کان شیئے	Be had Shukriya
身體	Shēntǐ	Health	صحت	شِین تھی	Sehat
禮貌	Lǐmào	Courteous	بااخلاق	لِی ماؤ	Ba Ikhlaq
客氣	Kèqì	Polite	نرم گو	کھہ چھی	Naram Go
別客氣	Bié kèqì	No mention (you are welcome)	تکلف نہ کرنا	پیئے کھہ چھی	Takaluf na karna
天	Tiān	Heaven	قُدرت	تھِیان	Qudrat
修理	Xiūlǐ	Repair	درست کرنا	شِیولی	Drust Karna
新聞	Xīnwén	News	خبر	شِن وین	Khabar
休息	Xiūxí	Rest	آرام	شِیو شی	Aram
加油	Jiāyóu	Cheer up	ہمت بڑھانا	چیایو	Heemat Barhana

Lesson-61

Common Words - عام الفاظ , Pǔtōng cí , 普通词Aam Alfaz

Chinese	Pinyin	English	اُردو	چینی تلفظ	Roman Urdu
邮票	Yóupiào	Stamp	ٹکٹ	یو پھیاو	Ticket
地址	Dìzhǐ	Address	پتہ	تی ژ	Pata
回信	Huíxìn	Reply	خط کا جواب	خوئی شِین	Khat Ka Jawab
信	Xìn	Letter	خط	شِین	Khat
立刻	Lìkè	Immedi-ately	فوراً	لی کھ	Forun
变化	Biànhuà	Change	بدلنا	پیان خوا	Badlna
自己	Zìjǐ	Self	خود	ذِی چی	Khud
又	Yòu	Again	دو بارہ	یو	Dobara
忽然	Hūrán	Suddenly	اچانک	خور آن	Achanak
热闹	Rènào	Excitement	گہما گہمی	رناو	Gahma gahmi
礼物	Lǐwù	Gift	تحفہ	لی اُو	Tuhfa
旅馆	Lǚguǎn	Hotel	ہوٹل	لوئی کو آن	Hotel
老	Lǎo	Old	بزرگ	لاو	Buzrg
研究	Yánjiū	Research	تحقیق	یان چیو	Tahqiq

Lesson-62

Common use sentences– عام استعمال جملے Pǔtōng jùzi，普通句子 Am Jumle

Chinese	Pinyin	English	اُردو	چینی تلفظ	Roman Urdu
你好	Nǐ hǎo	How do you do?	آپکا کیا حال ہے؟	نِی ہاو	Apka Kiya haal hai?
我很好	Wǒ hěn hǎo	I am alright	میں ٹھیک ہوں۔	و خین خاو	Mein theek hoon
你们好	Nǐmen hǎo	How are all of you?	آپ لوگ کیسے ہیں؟	نِی مین خاو	Ap log Kaise hain?
忙吗	Máng ma	Are you busy?	کیا آپ مصروف ہیں؟	نِی مانگ ما؟	Ap kiya Masroof hain?
你好吗	Nǐ hǎo ma	How are you?	آپ ٹھیک ہیں؟	نِی خاو ما؟	Ap theek hain?
很好	Hěn hǎo	Alright	بہت اچھا۔	خین خاو	Bahut Ach'a
谢谢你	Xièxiè nǐ	Thank you	آپ کا شکریہ۔	شیے شِی نِی۔	Ap ka Shukriya
你学习什么	Nǐ xuéxí shénme	What do you study?	اُپ کیا پڑھتے ہیں؟	نِی شوے شی شینما	Ap kiya parhte hain?
我学习汉语	Wǒ xuéxí hànyǔ	I study Chinese	میں چینی پڑھتا ہوں۔	وشوے شِی خانِوی۔	Mein Cheeni par-hta hoon

Lesson-63

Common use sentences– عام استعمال جملے Pǔtōng jùzi，普通句子 Am Jumle

Chinese	Pinyin	English	اُردو	چینی تلفظ	Roman Urdu
他学习什么	Tā xuéxí shénme	What does he/she study?	وہ کیاپڑھتا ہے؟	تھا شوے شِی شینما۔	Woh kiya parrhta hai?
他也学习汉语	Tā yě xuéxí hànyǔ	He also studies Chinese	وہ بھی چینی پڑھتا ہے۔	تھایے شوے شِی خانوی۔	Woh bhi Cheeni parrhta hai
汉语难吗	Hànyǔ nán ma	Is Chinese difficult?	کیا چینی مشکل ہے؟	خانوی نان ما؟	Kiya Cheeni Mushkil hai?
汉语不难	Hànyǔ bù nán	Chinese is not difficult	چینی مشکل نہیں۔	خانوی پُو نان۔	Cheeni mushkil nahee.
你做什么呢	Nǐ zuò shénme ne	What are you doing?	آپ کیا کر رہے ہو؟	نِی ذو شینمانہ۔	Ap kiya Kar rahe hain?
我写汉字呢	Wǒ xiě hànzì ní	I am writing Chinese	میں چینی لکھ رہا ہوں۔	وشیے خانذی نہ۔	Mein Cheeni Likh raha hoon
他做什么呢	Tā zuò shénme ne	What is he doing?	وہ کیا کر رہا ہے؟	تھا ذو شِینما نہ۔	Woh kiya kar raha hai?

Chinese	Pinyin	English	اُردو	چینی تلفظ	Roman Urdu
他们做什么呢	Tāmen zuò shénme ne	What are they doing?	وہ لوگ کیا کر رہے ہیں۔	تھامین ذو شینما نہ۔	Woh log kiya kar rahe hain?

*In China, out of respect, those who are older are addressed old as 'Lâo' with their name and those who are younger,are addressed young as 'Xiao'. For example Lâo Li and Xiăo Wang. Calling one by name alone, is discourteous, disrespectful and un-chinese.

Lesson-64

Common use sentences– عام استعمال جملے Pǔtōng jùzi，普通句子 Am Jumle

Chinese	Pinyin	English	اُردو	چینی تلفظ	Roman Urdu
这是书吗	Zhè shì shū ma	Is this a book?	کیا یہ کتاب ہے؟	ژشِی شُوما	Kiya yeh kitab hai?
这是书	Zhè shì shū	This is a book	یہ کتاب ہے۔	ژشِی شُو۔	Yeh kitab hai.
那是报纸吗	Nà shì bàozhǐ ma	Is that a newspa-per?	کیا وہ اخبار ہے؟	ناشِی پاو ما	Kiya woh Ikhbar hai?
那时报纸	Nà shí bàozhǐ	That is a newspaper	وہ اخبار ہے	ناشِی پاو ژ	Woh Ikh-bar hai.
那是什么	Nà shì shénme	What is that?	وہ کیا ہے	ناشِی شینما	Woh kiya hai?
那是画报	Nà shì huàbào	That is pictorial	وہ رسالہ ہے	ناشِی خوا پاو	Woh Risal hai.
他是老师吗	Tā shì lǎoshī ma	Is he/she a teacher?	کیا وہ استاد ہے؟	تھاشِی لاوشِی ما	Kiya Woh Ustad hai?
他不是老师	Tā bùshì lǎoshī	He/she is not a teacher	وہ استاد نہیں ہے	تھاپُوشِی لاوشِی	Woh Ustad Nahe Hai.

Lesson-65

Dialogue – مُکالمہ Duìhuà，对话 Mukalma

Chinese	Pinyin	English	اُردو	چینی تلفظ	Roman Urdu
他是哪国人	Tā shì nǎ guórén	Where is he from?	وہ کہاں کا رہنے والا ہے؟	تھا شی نا گو آرین	Woh kahan ka rahne wala hai?
他是中国人	Tā shì zhōngguó rén	He is Chi-nese	وہ چین کا رہنے والا ہے۔	تھا شی چونگہ ارین	Woh Cheen ka rahne wala hai.
我是巴基斯坦人	Wǒ shì bājīsītǎn rén	I am a Pakistani	میں پاکستانی ہوں	وشی پاچستھان رین	Mein Paki-stani hoon.
你叫什么名字	Nǐ jiào shénme míngzì	What is your name?	اُپکا کیا نام ہے	نی چیاو شینما مینگزہ	Apka kiya nam hai?
我叫 。	Wǒ jiào.	My name is...	میرا نام ہے---	وچیاو--	Mera nam ...hai

Chinese	Pinyin	English	اُردو	چینی تلفظ	Roman Urdu
他叫	Tā jiào	His/her name is	اس کا نام۔۔۔۔ہے	تا چیاؤ۔۔	Us ka nam...hai
请来	Qǐng lái	Please come	مہربانی آئیں	چھنگ لائی	Meharnba-ni ayain
请进	Qǐng jìn	Please come in	مہربانی اندر آئیں	چھنگ چِن	Meharba-ni under ayain
请坐	Qǐng zuò	Please sit down	مہربانی بیٹھیے	چھنگ زُوو	Meharbani baith'ye
请喝茶	Qǐng hē chá	Please drink tea	مہربانی چائے پیجیے	چھنگ خاچھا	Mehar-bani Chai peej'ye

Lesson-66

Dialogue– مُکالمہ Duìhuà，对话 Mukalma

Chinese	Pinyin	English	اُردو	چینی تلفظ	Roman Urdu
你怎么样	Nǐ Zěnme yàng	How is it with you?	آپ ٹھیک ہیں نا؟	نِی ذِمایانگ	Ap kaise hain?
太谢谢	Tài xièxiè	Thank you very much	بہت بہت شکریہ	تھائی شیے شی	Bahut Bahut shukriya
你去哪里	Nǐ qù nǎlǐ	Where did you go?	آپ کہاں گے تھے؟	نِی چھوئی نالی	Ap kahan ga'ye teh.
我去中国	Wǒ qù zhōngguó	I went to China	میں چین گیا تھا	و چھوی چونگو آ	Mein Cheen gaya tah.
他去巴基斯坦了	Tā qù bā-jīsītǎnle	He went to Pakistan	وہ پاکستان گیا ہے	تا چھوی پاچستھان لہ	Woh Paki-stan gaya hai.
今天你怎么样	Jīntiān nǐ zěnme yàng	How are you today?	آج آپ کیسے ہیں؟	چن تھیان نِی ذمہ یانگ	Aj ap kaise hain?
巴基斯坦怎么样	Bājīsītǎn zěnme yàng	How is Pakistan?	پاکستان کیسا ہے؟	پاچستھان ذمہ یانگ	Pakistan kaisa hai?
巴基斯坦很好	Bājīsītǎn hěn hǎo	Pakistan is very good	پاکستان بہت اچھا ہے	پاچستھان خین خاو	Pakistan bahut acha hai
那儿很好	Nà'er hěn hǎo	It is very good there	وہاں بہت اچھا ہے	نار خین خاون	Wahan bahut acha hai.

Lesson-67

Dialogue – مُکالمہ Liáotiān，聊天 Mukalma

Chinese	Pinyin	English	اُردو	چینی تلفظ	Roman Urdu
中国怎么样	Zhōngguó zěnme yàng	How is China?	چین کیسا ہے؟	چونگہ آزمہ یانگ	Cheen kaisa hai?
中国很好	Zhōngguó hěn hǎo	China is very good	چین بہت اچھا ہے۔	چونگہ آخین خاو	Cheen bahut acha hai.
那儿很好	Nà'er hěn hǎo	It is very good there	وہاں بہت اچھا ہے	نار خین خاو	Wahan bahut acha hai.
巴基斯坦 - 中国	Bājīsītǎn - zhōngguó	Pakistan and China	پاکستان اور چین	پاچستھان، چونگوآ	Pakistan aur Cheen
朋友，兄弟，邻居，同伴	Péngyǒu, xiōngdì, línjū, tóng-bàn	Friends, Brothers, Neigh-bours, Partners	دوست، بھائی، پڑوسی، ساتھی	تھونگ پڑ، لینگ چوئی، شیونگ ڈِی، پھانگ یو	Dost bhai parosi sathi

Lesson-68

Conversation – بات چیت Liáotiān，聊天 Ba'at Cheet

Chinese	Pinyin	English	اُردو	چینی تلفظ	Roman Urdu
你去哪儿	Nǐ qù nǎ'er	Where are you going?	آپ کہاں جارہے ہیں؟	نِی چھوئی نار	Ap kahan jarahe hain?
我去巴基斯坦	Wǒ qù bājīsītǎn	I am going to Pakistan	میں پاکستان جارہا ہوں۔	وچھوئی پاجستھان	Mein Pakistan jar aha hoon.
他们去哪儿	Tāmen qù nǎ'er	Where are they going?	وہ لوگ کہاں جارہے ہیں؟	تھامین چھوئی نار	Woh log kahan jara-he hain?
他们去中国	Tāmen qù zhōngguó	They are going to China	وہ لوگ چین جا رہے ہیں	تھامین چھوئی چونگو آ	Woh log Cheen jara-he hain.
你是哪里人	Nǐ shì nǎlǐ rén	Where are you from?	آپ لوگ کہاں سے ہیں؟	نِی شی نالی رین	Ap log kahan se hain?
我是巴基斯坦人	Wǒ shì bājīsītǎn rén	I am a Pakistani	میں پاکستانی ہوں	و شی پاچستھان رین	Mein Paki-stani hoon.
他是哪里人	Tā shì nǎlǐ rén	Where is he / she from?	وہ کہاں سے ہے؟	تھاشی نالی رین	Woh kahan se hai?
他是中国人	Tā shì zhōngguó rén	He is from China	وہ چین سے ہیں	تھا شی چونگو آ رین	Woh Cheen se hain.

Lesson-69

Conversation – بات چیت Liáotiān，聊天 Ba'at Cheet

Chinese	Pinyin	English	اُردو	چینی تلفظ	Roman Urdu
你家有几口人	Nǐ jiā yǒu jǐ kǒu rén	How many family members do you have?	آپکے خاندان میں کتنے افراد ہیں؟	نی چیایو ۔ چی کھورین	Apke khandan me kitne log hain?
我家有四口人	Wǒjiā yǒu sì kǒu rén	My family has four members	میرے خاندان میں چار افراد ہیں	وچیایو سی کھو رین	Mere khandan me char ifrad hain.
你的爸爸做什么	Nǐ de bà ba zuò shénme	What does your father do?	آپ کے والد کیا کرتے ہیں؟	نِی پاپا ذُو شینما	Apke walid kiya karte hain?
我的爸爸是老师	Wǒ de bà ba shì lǎoshī	My father is a teacher	میرے والد استاد ہیں	و پاپاشی لاو شی	Meray walid Ustad hain.
她的姐姐是大夫	Tā de jiejie shì dàfū	Her sister is a doctor	اس کی بہن ڈاکٹر ہے	تھا چے چے شی تَائی فوَ	Uski bahan doctor hai.
我的哥哥是学生	Wǒ dí gēgē shì xuéshēng	My elder brother is a student	میرا بڑا بھائی طالب علم ہے۔	وِکہ گہ شی شُوے سنگ	Mera bara bhai talib ilm hai.
我的妈妈在大学教书	Wǒ de māmā zài dàxué jiāoshū	My mother teaches in a university	میری ماں جامعہ میں پڑھاتی ہے۔	و ماما ذاے تاشوے چیاو شُو	Mery ma jame'a me parhati hain.

Lesson-70

Learning language – زبان کی تعلیم Xué yǔyán ، 学语言 Zaban ki ta'alim

Chinese	Pinyin	English	اُردو	چینی تلفظ	Roman Urdu
我是学生	Wǒ shì xuéshēng	I am a student	میں طالب علم ہوں	و شی شُوے شنگ	Mein talib ilm hoon.
他是大夫	Tā shì dàfū	He is a doctor	وہ ڈاکٹر ہے	تھا شِی تاءفو	Woh doc-tor hai.
你在哪儿学习	Nǐ zài nǎ'er xuéxí	Where do you study?	آپ کہاں پڑھتے ہیں؟	نِی ذاے نآر شُوے شِی	Ap kahan parrhte hain?
我在北京大学学习	Wǒ zài běijīng dàxué xuéxí	I study in Beijing University	میں جامعہ بیجنگ میں پڑھتا ہوں	وذاے پیچنگ تاشُوے شُوے شِی	Mein Jam'ea Beijing me parrhta hoon.
你学习什么	Nǐ xuéxí shénme	What do you study?	آپ کیا پڑھتے ہیں؟	نِی شوے شِی شینما	Ap kiya par'rhte hain?
我学习乌尔都语	Wǒ xuéxí wū ěr dū yǔ	I study Urdu	میں اردو پڑھتا ہوں	وشُوے شِی اُوردو یوی	Mein Urdu parrhta hoon.

Lesson-71

Learning language – زبان کی تعلیم Xué yǔyán，学语言 Zaban ki ta'alim

Chinese	Pinyin	English	اُردو	چینی تلفظ	Roman Urdu
他学习什么	Tā xuéxí shénme	What does he study?	وہ کیا پڑھتا ہے؟	تھا شُوے شی شینما	Woh kiya par'rhta hai?
他学习汉语	Tā xuéxí hànyǔ	He studies Chinese	وہ چینی پڑھتا ہے	تھا شُوے شی خانوی	Woh Cheeni par'rhta hai
现在上课	Xiànzài shàngkè	Now we begin classes	اب سبق کا آغاز کریں	شیان ذاے شنگ کھ	Ab sabaq ka agaz kare'in.
听我发音	Tīng wǒ fāyīn	Listen to my pronounciation	میرے لہجہ کو غور کریں	تھنگ و فاین	Mere lahje ko gor kare'in
再听一遍	Zài tīng yībiàn	Listen to it again	اِسے دوبارہ سنیں	ذاے تھنگ اِی پیان	Ise dobar-ah sune'in.
再说一遍	Zàishuō yībiàn	Say it again	اِسے دوبارہ بولیں	ذاے شُواِی پیان	Ise dobar-ah bole'in.
跟我说	Gēn wǒ shuō	Say it with me	میرے ساتھ بولیں	کین و شُوو	Mere sa'ath bole'in.
一边说，一边听	Yībiān shuō, yībiān tīng	Listen and tell	سنیں اور بولیں	اِی پیان شُوو۔ اِی پیان تھنگ	Sune'in Aur bole'in

Lesson-72

Friends Conversation – دوستانہ گفتگو Liáotiān，聊天 Dostana guftagu

Chinese	Pinyin	English	اُردو	چینی تلفظ	Roman Urdu
你好	Nǐ hǎo	How do you do?	آپ کا کیا حال ہے؟	نی ہاو	Ap ka kiya haal hai?
你去哪儿了	Nǐ qù nǎerle	Where did you go?	آپ کہاں گئے ہوے تھے؟	نِی چُھوئی نار لا	Ap kahan Gaye huye teh?
我去中国了	Wǒ qù zhōngguóle	I had gone to China	میں چین گیا ہوا تھا	و چھوئی چونگو آ لا	Mein Cheen gaya hua tah.
她去哪儿了	Tā qù nǎerle	Where has she gone?	وہ کہاں گئی ہوئی ہیں؟	تھا چھوئی نارلا	Woh kahan gayi hui hain?
他去巴基斯坦了	Tā qù bā-jīsītǎnle	She has gone to Pakistan	وہ پاکستان گئی ہوئی ہیں	تھا چھوئی پاچستھان لا	Woh Paki-stan gayi hui hai.

Chinese	Pinyin	English	اُردو	چینی تلفظ	Roman Urdu
你在中国捉什么	Nǐ zài zhōngguó zhuō shénme	What do you do in China?	آپ چین میں کیا کرتے ہیں؟	نِی ذاے چونگو آ ذو شینما	Ap Cheen me kiya karte hain?
我在中国做工	Wǒ zài zhōngguó zuògōng	I work in China.	میں چین میں کام کرتا ہوں	و ذاے چونگو آ ذُو کونگ	Mein Cheen me kam karta hoon.
他们在巴基斯坦做什么	Tāmen zài bājīsītǎn zuò shénme	What do they do in Pakistan?	وہ پاکستان میں کیا کرتے ہیں؟	تھا مین ذاے پاچستھان ذو شینما	Woh Pakistan me kiya karte hain?

Lesson-73

Friends Conversation – دوستانہ گفتگو Liáotiān ، 聊天 Dostana guftagu

Chinese	Pinyin	English	اُردو	چینی تلفظ	Roman Urdu
您学习中文吗	Nín xuéxí zhōngwén ma	Do you study Chinese?	کیا آپ چینی پڑھتے ہیں؟	نِی شُوے شی چونگ وین ما	Kiya ap Cheeni par'rhte hain?
我学习中文	Wǒ xuéxí zhōngwén	I study Chinese	میں چینی پڑھتا ہوں	وُشُوے شی چونگ وین	Mein Cheeni par'rhta hoon.
中文难吗	Zhōngwén nán ma	Is Chinese hard?	کیا چینی مشکل ہے؟	چونگ وین نان ما	Kiya Cheeni mushkil hai?
中文不太难	Zhōngwén bù tài nán	Chinese is not very difficult	چینی زیادہ مشکل نہیں ہے	چونگ وین پُو تھائی نان	Cheeni ziyada mushkil nahee hai.
乌尔都语难吗	Wū ěr dū yǔ nán ma	Is Urdu difficult?	کیا اردو مشکل ہے؟	اِوردو یوی نان ما	Kiya Urdu mushkil hai?
乌尔都语不太难	Wū ěr dū yǔ bù tài nán	Urdu is not very difficult	اردو زیادہ مشکل نہیں ہے	اوردو یوی پُو تھائی نان	Urdu ziya-da mushkil nahee.

Lesson-74

Introduction – تعارف کرنا Jièshào，介绍 Ta'aruf karna

Chinese	Pinyin	English	اُردو	چینی تلفظ	Roman Urdu
您是谁	Nín shì shuí	Who are you?	آپ کون ہیں؟	نِی شِی شوئی	Ap ko'n hain?
我是贾韦德	Wǒ shì jiǎwéidé	I am Javed	میں جاوید ہوں	وُ شِی جاویدا	Mein Javed hoon.
他是谁	Tā shì shuí	Who is he/ she?	وہ کون ہے؟	تھا شِی شوئی	Woh k'on hai?
他是我的中各国朋友	Tā shì wǒ de zhōng gèguó péngyǒu	He is my Chinese friend	وہ میرا چینی دوست ہے	تھا شِی و دا چونگو آ پھانگ یو	Woh mera Cheeni dost hai.
他是你的巴基斯坦朋友吗	Tā shì nǐ de bājīsītǎn péngyǒu ma	Is he/ she your Pakistani friend?	کیا وہ تمہارا پاکستانی دوست ہے؟	تھا شِی نِی دا پاچستھان پھانگ یو ما	Kiya woh tumhara Pakistani dost hai?
他叫社么名字	Tā jiào shè me míngzì	What is his/her name?	اس کا کیا نام ہے	تھا چیاو شینما منگزہ	Us ka kiya nam hai?
他叫哈桑	Tā jiào hā sāng	His name is Hasan	اس کا نام حسن ہے	تھا چِیاو حسن	Us ka nam Hasan hai.

Lesson-75

Introduction –تعارف کرنا Jièshào，介绍 Ta'aruf Karna

Chinese	Pinyin	English	اُردو	چینی تلفظ	Roman Urdu
您认识他吗	Nín rènshi tā ma	Do you know him?	کیا آپ اُنہیں جانتے ہیں؟	نِی رین شِی تھا ما	Kiya ap Unhe jante hain?
我认识他	Wǒ rènshi tā	I know him	میں اُن کو جانتا ہوں	ورین شِی تھا	Mein Un ko Janta hoon.
你的朋友北京人吗	Nǐ de péngyǒu běijīng rén ma	Is your friend from Beijing?	کیا آپ کا دوست بیجنگ سے ہے؟	نِی دا پھانگ یو پیجنگ رین ما	Kiya apka dost Bei-jing se hai
不是，他是上海人	Bùshì, tā shì shàng-hǎi rén	No, he is from Shanghai	نہیں وہ شنگھائی سے ہے	بوِ شِی، تا شِی شنگھائی رین	Nahee,wo shanghai se hai.
他叫小李	Tā jiào xiǎo li	His name is Xiao Li	اس کا نام شیاو لی ہے	تھاچیاو شیاو لی	Us ka nam Xiao Li hai

Chinese	Pinyin	English	اُردو	چینی تلفظ	Roman Urdu
我问，你回答	Wǒ wèn, nǐ huídá	I ask, you reply	میں پوچھوں، آپ جواب دیں	ووین نِی خوئی تا	Mein puchu'n ap jawab dein.
对不对	Duì bùduì	Is it right?	کیا یہ ٹھیک ہے؟	توئی پُو توئی	Kiya yeh theek hai?
不对	Bùduì	No, it is not right	نہیں یہ ٹھیک نہیں ہے	پو تُوئی	Nahee yeh theek nahee hai.

Lesson-76

Family – خاندان Jiā ، 家 Khan'daan

Chinese	Pinyin	English	اُردو	چینی تلفظ	Roman Urdu
您爱人做什么	Nín àirén zuò shénme	What does your wife do?	آپ کی بیگم کیا کرتی ہیں؟	نی آءرین ڈُو شینما	Ap ki begum kiya karti hain?
我爱人在家里做工	Wǒ àirén zài jiālǐ zuògōng	My wife works at home.	میری بیگم گھر میں کام کرتی ہیں	و آءرین ذاے چیا لی کونگ ذو	Meri be-gum ghar me kam karti hain.
她叫什么名字	Tā jiào shénme míngzì	What is her name?	ان کا کیا نام ہے؟	تھا چیاو شینما مینگزہ	Un ka kiya nam hai?
她叫沙娜兹	Tā jiào shā nà zī	Her name is Shahnaz.	اُن کا نام شہناز ہے	تھا چیاو شہنازا	Un ka nam Shahnaz hai.
您爱人叫什么	Nín àirén jiào shénme	What is your wife's name?	آپ کی بیگم کا کیا نام ہے؟	نِی آءرین چیاو شینما	Ap ki begum ka kiya nam hai?
他叫王女士	Tā jiào wáng nǚshì	Her name is Mrs. Wang.	ان کا نام مسز وانگ ہے	تھا چیاو وانگ نِو شی	Un ka nam mrs. Wang hai.

Lesson-77

Family – خاندان Jiā ，家 Khan daan

Chinese	Pinyin	English	اُردو	چینی تلفظ	Roman Urdu
你有几个孩子	Nǐ yǒu jǐ gè háizi	How many children do you have?	آپ کے بچے کتنے ہیں؟	نی یو چی گا ہاءزہ	Ap ke ketne bache hain?
我有四个孩子	Wǒ yǒu sì gè háizi	I have four children.	میرے چار بچے ہیں	ویو سِیگہ ہاءزہ	Mere char bache hain.
他有两个孩子	Tā yǒu liǎng gè háizi	He has two children.	اس کے دو بچے ہیں؟	تھا یو لیانگا ہاءزہ	Us ke do bache hain.
一个男孩，一个女孩	Yīgè nán-hái, yīgè nǚhái	One son, one daugh-ter	ایک بیٹا، ایک بیٹی	ایگا نان ہر، ایگا نِو ہر	Ek beta, ek betty
他们在哪儿学习	Tāmen zài nǎer xuéxí	Where do they study?	وہ کہاں پڑھتے ہیں؟	تھا مین ذاے نار شوے شی	Wo kahan par'rhte hain?

Chinese	Pinyin	English	اُردو	چینی تلفظ	Roman Urdu
他们比较小	Tāmen bǐjiào xiǎo	They are relatively small.	وہ ابھی تھوڑے چھوٹے ہیں	تھا مین پی چیاو شیاو	Woh abhi thorre chote hain.
他们在小学学习	Tāmen zài xiǎoxué xuéxí	They study in Primary School.	وہ لوگ پرائمری سکول میں پڑھتے ہیں	تھا مین ذاے شیاو شوے شوے شی	Woh log primary school me par'rhte hain

Lesson-78

Family – خاندان Jiā ， 家 Khan daan

Chinese	Pinyin	English	اُردو	چینی تلفظ	Roman Urdu
您家有什么人	Nín jiā yǒu shén me rén	Who else are in your family?	آپ کے خاندان میں کون لوگ ہیں؟	نی چیا ہای یو شینما رین	Apke khan-daan me ko'n log hain?
我家有爸爸，妈妈，哥哥	Wǒjiā yǒu bà ba, māmā, gēgē	In my fam-ily, there is my father, mother and elder brother.	میرے خاندان میں والد، والدہ اور بڑے بھائی ہیں۔	وہ چیا یو پا پا، ما ما، گا گا۔	Mere khandaan me abbu, Ammi aur bare bhai hain.
还有谁	Hái yǒu shuí	Who else are in your family?	اور کون کون ہیں؟	ہائی یو شوئی	Aur ko'n ko'n hain?
还有爷爷，奶奶	Hái yǒu yéye, nǎinai	I have a grandad and grand-ma.	اور دادا دادی ہیں	ہائی یو یہ یے، نائی نائی	Aur dada, dadi hain.
他们都在巴基斯坦	Tāmen dōu zài bājīsītǎn	They are all in Pakistan.	وہ سب پاکستان میں ہیں	تھا مین طو ذاے پاچستھان	Woh sab Pakistan me hain.

Chinese	Pinyin	English	اُردو	چینی تلفظ	Roman Urdu
你朋友家在上海吗	Nǐ péngyǒu jiā zài shànghǎi ma	Is your friend's family in Shanghai?	کیا تمہارے دوست کا خاندان شنگھائی میں ہے؟	نِی پھانگ یو چیاذاے شنگھائی ما	Kiya tumhare dostka Khandaan Shanghai me hai?
不是，他们在北京	Bùshì, tāmen zài běijīng	No, they are in Bei-jing.	نہیں وہ بیجنگ میں ہیں	پُو شِی، تھا مین ذاے پیجنگ	Nahee Woh BeiJing me Hain.

Lesson-79

Embassy – سفارتخانہ Dàshǐ guǎn， 大使馆 Safarat Khana

Chinese	Pinyin	English	اُردو	چینی تلفظ	Roman Urdu
今天我们去大使馆	Jīntiān wǒmen qù dàshǐ guǎn	Today we will go to the Embassy.	آج ہم سفارت خانہ جائیں گے	چِن تھیان ومین چھوئی تاشی کو آن	Aj hum safarat khana ja'enge
大使要会见我们	Dàshǐ yào huìjiàn wǒmen	The Ambassador wishes to see us.	سفیر صاحب ہم سب سے ملاقات کریں گے	تاشی یاو خوئی چیان ومین	Safir sahib hum sab se mulaqa'at karein ge
我们跟大使握手	Wǒmen gēn dàshǐ wòshǒu	We will shake hands with the Ambassador.	ہم لوگ سفیر صاحب سے ہاتھ ملائیں گے	ومین کین تاشی وشاو	Hum log safir sahib se haath milayenge
巴基斯坦和中国好朋友	Bājīsītǎn hé zhōngguó hǎo péngyǒu	Pakistan and China are good friends.	پاکستان اور چین اچھے دوست ہیں	پاچستھان خہ چونگو آ خاو پھانگ یو	Pakistan aur Cheen ache dost hain.
我们加强友谊	Wǒmen jiāqiáng yǒuyì	We strengthen the friendship.	ہم لوگ دوستی بڑھاتے ہیں	ومین چیا چھیانگ یُو اِی	Hum log dosti barhate hain.

Chinese	Pinyin	English	اُردو	چینی تلفظ	Roman Urdu
我们互相帮组，增进团结	Wǒmen hùxiāng bāng zǔ, zēngjìn tuánjié	We help each other, strengthen unity.	ہم لوگ ایک دوسرے کی مدد کرتے اور اتحاد بڑھاتے ہیں	ومین خوشیانگ پانگ تواذنگ چِن تھو آن چے	Hum log ek dusre ki madad karte aur ittehad barhate hain.

Lesson-80

Shopping – شاپنگ Mǎi dōngxi，买东西 Kharid Farokht

Chinese	Pinyin	English	اُردو	چینی تلفظ	Roman Urdu
小姐：先生，您要什么？	Xiǎojiě: Xiān-shēng, nín yào shénme?	Miss: Sir, what do you want?	خاتون: جناب آپ کو کیا چاہیے؟	شِیایوچے: شیان شنگ نی یاو شینما	Khatoon: Janab apko kiya chah'iye
顾客：我要买这个杂志。	Gùkè: Wǒ yāomǎi zhège zázhì.	Customer: I want to buy this magazine.	خریدار: میں یہ رسالہ خریدنا چاہتا ہوں۔	کُوکھہ: ویاو مائی چیگاذاٹر	Kharidar: Mein yeh ri-sala khareed-na chahta hoon.
小姐：先生，你还想买什么？	Xiǎojiě: Xiānshēng, nǐ hái xiǎng mǎi shénme?	Miss: Sir, what else are you thinking to buy?	خاتون: جناب اور آپ کیا خریدنا چاہتے ہیں؟	شیاوچے: نی ہاے شیانگ مائی شینما	Khatoon: Janab aur ap kiya khareed-na chahte hain?
售货员：你要买什么？	Shòuhuòyuán: Nǐ yāomǎi shénme?	Salesman: What do you want to buy?	سیلزپرسن: آپ کیا خریدنا چاہتے ہیں؟	شوخو یوآن: نِی یاو مائی شینما	Salesper-son: Ap kiya khareedna chahte hain?
先生：哪个都很好看	Xiānshēng: Nǎge dōu hěn hǎokàn	Gentleman: Those all very good.	جناب: وہ سارے بہت خوبصورت ہیں	شیان شنگ: نہ گہ توِ خین خاو کھن	Janab: Woh sare bahut khubsurat hain.
小姐：你要那个？	Xiǎojiě: Nǐ yào nàgè?	Miss: you want them?	خاتون: آپ کو وہ سب چاہیے؟	شیاوجیے: نِی یاؤ نہ گہ	Khatoon: Ap ko woh sab chahiye.
顾客：多少钱？	Gùkè: Duōshǎo qián?	Customer: what is the price?	خریدار: کتنی قیمت ہے؟	کُوکھہ: تُوو شاو چھیان	Kha-reed-ar:ketni qimathai?

Lesson-81

Shopping – شاپنگ Mǎi dōngxi，买东西Kharid Farokht

Chinese	Pinyin	English	اُردو	چینی تلفظ	Roman Urdu
先生：这个很贵	Xiānshēng: Zhège hěn guì	Gentleman: This is very expensive.	جناب: یہ بہت مہنگا ہے	شیان شنگ: چیگا خین کوئی	Janab: Yeh bahut mahnga hai.
售货员：不贵	Shòuhuòyuán: Bù guì	Salesperson: It is not expensive.	سیلزپرسن: بالکل مہنگا نہیں	شوخویو آن: پُوگوئی	Salesperson: bilkul mahnga nahee.
顾客：你又便宜的吗？	Gùkè: Nǐ yòu piányi de ma?	Customer: Do you have cheaper ones?	خریدار: کیا آپ کے پاس سستے والا ہے؟	کُو کھہ: نِی یُو پھیان اِی ما	Khareedar: kiya ap ke pas saste wala hai?
小姐：有，很多便宜的。	Xiǎojiě: Yǒu, hěnduō piányi de.	Miss: Yes, I have many cheap ones.	خاتون: ہاں میرے پاس بہت سستے والا ہے	شیاو جیے: یو خین تُو و پھیان اِی	Khatoon: ha'an merepa-s bahut sastewa-la hai.

Chinese	Pinyin	English	اُردو	چینی تلفظ	Roman Urdu
先生：请你给我看一下	Xiānshēng: Qǐng nǐ gěi wǒ kàn yīxià	Gentle-man: Please show me so for a while.	جناب: آپ مجھے کچھ دیر کے لیے دکھائیں گے	شیان شنگ: چھِنگ نِی کے اِی وکھن اِی شِیا	Janab: mujhe kuch derkelie dekhainge?
售货员：您等一会儿。	Shòuhuòyuán: Nín děng yīhuǐ'er.	Sales-person: Would you please wait a minute?	سیلز پرسن: آپ تھوڑی دیر انتظار کریں	شوخویو آن: نِن تنگ اِی خووَر	Salesper-son:Ap thorider intizar karein

Lesson-82

Seeing a Doctor – ڈاکٹر سے گفتگو Kàn Bìng, 看病 Doctor se guftagu

Chinese	Pinyin	English	اُردو	چینی تلفظ	Roman Urdu
大夫：阿里先生，您怎么了？	Dàifū: Ālǐ xiānshēng, nín zěnme?	Doctor: Mr. Ali, how are you?	ڈاکٹر: علی صاحب آپ کیسے ہیں؟	دائیفو: عالی شیان شنگ، نین ذین ما لہ؟	Doctor: Ali sahib ap kaise hain?
阿里：我不舒服。	Ālǐ: Wǒ bú shūfú.	Ali: I am not feeling well.	علی: میری طبیعت خراب ہے	عالی: وو پو شوفو۔	Ali: Meri tabyiat kharab hai.
大夫：您怎么不舒服？	Dàifū: Nín zěnme bú shūfú?	Doctor: How do you feel ill?	ڈاکٹر: آپ کو کہاں تکلیف ہے؟	دائیفو: نین ذینما پو شوفو؟	Doctor: Ap ko kahan takleef hai?
阿里：我又头疼发烧。	Ālǐ: Wǒ yòu tóuténg fāshāo.	Ali: I have a headache and fever.	علی: میرے سر میں درد اور بخار ہے	عالی: وو یو ٹھوتھنگ فاشاو۔	Ali: Mere sar me dard aur bukhar hai.
大夫：你还有什么问题？	Dàifū: Nǐ hái yǒu shé me wèntí?	Doctor: What other problems do you have?	ڈاکٹر: اس کے علاوہ اور کیا تکلیف ہے؟	دائیفو: نی حاے یو شین ما وین تی؟	Doctor: Is ke ilawa aur kiya takleef hai?

Lesson-83

Seeing a Doctor – ڈاکٹر سے گفتگو Kàn Bìng, 看病 Doctor se guftagu

Chinese	Pinyin	English	اُردو	چینی تلفظ	Roman Urdu
阿里：我睡不好。	Ālǐ: Wǒ shuì bù hǎo.	Ali: I can not sleep	علی: مجھے نیند نہیں آتی	عالی: وو شوی پو خاو۔	Ali: Mujhe neend nahee a'ati.
大夫：你张开嘴，我看看。	Dàifū: Nǐ zhāng kāi zuǐ, wǒ kàn kàn.	Doctor: You open your mouth, I want to see.	ڈاکٹر: آپ منہ کھولیں، میں دیکھنا چاہتا ہوں	دائفو: نی چانگ کای ذوی، وو کن کن۔	Doctor: Ap munh kholein, mein dekhna chahta hoon.
阿里：我是不是感冒了？	Ālǐ: Wǒ shì bùshì gǎnmàole?	Ali: Have I got flu?	علی: کیا مجھے ذکام ہو گیا ہے؟	عالی: وو شی پوشی گن ماولی؟	Ali: kiya mujhe zukam hogaya hai?

Chinese	Pinyin	English	اُردو	چینی تلفظ	Roman Urdu
大夫：阿里，你觉得怎么样？	Dàifū: Ālǐ, nǐ juéde zěnme yàng?	Doctor: Ali, how do you feel?	ڈاکٹر: علی تم کیسا محسوس کر رہے ہو؟	دائیفو: عالی، نی چوی داذین ما یانگ؟	Doctor: Ali tum kaisa mahsus kar rahe ho?
阿里：我觉得不太好。	Ālǐ: Wǒ jué dé bù tài hǎo.	Ali: I am not feel-ing well.	علی: میں اچھا محسوس نہیں کر رہا ہوں	عالی: وو چوی داپو تای خاو۔	Mein acha mahsus nahee karraha hoon.

Lesson-84

Seeing a Doctor – ڈاکٹر سے گفتگو Kàn Bìng, 看病 Doctor se guftagu

Chinese	Pinyin	English	اُردو	چینی تلفظ	Roman Urdu
大夫：你有什么问题？	Dàifū: Nǐyǒu shé me wèntí?	Doctor: What problem do you have?	ڈاکٹر: آپ کو کیا مسئلہ ہے؟	دائیفو: نی یو شین ما وین تی ؟	Doctor: Ap Ko kiya ma-sla hai?
阿里：我呼吸不好。	Ālǐ: Wǒ hūxī bù hǎo.	Ali: I have breathing problem, heart beats fast.	علی: میری سانس ٹھیک نہیں ہے، دل تیز دھڑکتا ہے	عالی: وہ خوشی پو خاو۔	Ali: Meri-sa'ns th-eek nahee hai.
大夫：你有这个病几天了？	Dàifū: Nǐ yǒu zhège bìng jǐ tiānle?	Doctor: Since when, you have this sickness?	ڈاکٹر: آپ کو یہ بیماری کب سے ہے؟	دائیفو: نی یو چیگا پنگ چی تھیان لہ ؟	Doctor: Ap ko yeh bimari kab se hai?

Chinese	Pinyin	English	اُردو	چینی تلفظ	Roman Urdu
阿里：好几天了大概三个月。	Ālǐ: Hǎojǐ tiānle dàgài sān gè yuè.	Ali: A few days have passed. Roughly three months.	علی: چند روز ہو گئے، تقریباً تین ماہ	عالی: خاوجی تھیان لہ داگای سن گا یوے۔	Ali: Chand Roz ho gaye taqreeban teen mah.
大夫：你需要全面检查。	Dàifū: Nǐ xūyào quán-miàn jiǎnchá.	Doctor: You need a detailed check-up.	ڈاکٹر: آپ کو تفصیلی معاءنہ کی ضرورت ہے	دایفو: نی شو یاو چھوآن میان چیان ٹھا۔	Doctor: Ap ko tafseeli Muaene ki Zaroorat Hai.

Lesson-85

Seeing a Doctor – ڈاکٹر سے گفتگو Kàn Bìng, 看病 Doctor se guftagu

Chinese	Pinyin	English	اُردو	چینی تلفظ	Roman Urdu
大夫：阿里，你今天怎么了？	Dàifū: Ālǐ, nǐ jīntiān zěnmele?	Doctor: Ali, How are you to-day?	ڈاکٹر: علی آج آپ کا کیا حال ہے؟	دایفو: عالی، نی چن تھیان زین ما لہ؟	Doctor: Ali Apka kiya haal hai?
阿里：我昏迷了我的手疼。	Ālǐ: Wǒ hūn-míle wǒ de shǒu téng.	Ali: I fell uncon-scious. My hand is aching.	علی: میں بے ہوش ہو گیا تھا، میرا ہاتھ درد کر رہا ہے	عالی: وو خون ملا وو دا شو تھنگ۔	Ali: mein Behosh hogaya tah,mera haath dard horaha hai.
大夫：你还在哪儿疼？	Dàifū: Nǐ hái zài nà téng?	Doctor: Where else you have pain?	ڈاکٹر: آپ کو اور کہاں درد ہو رہا ہے؟	دایفو: نی حائی ذای نار تھنگ؟	Doctor: Ap ko aur kahan dard hora hai.

Chinese	Pinyin	English	اُردو	چینی تلفظ	Roman Urdu
阿里：我的眼睛，嗓子，肚子，嘴和全身有问题。	Ālǐ: Wǒ de yǎnjīng, sǎngzi, dùzi, zuǐ hé quánshēn yǒu wèntí.	Ali: My eyes, throat, stomach, mouth and whole body have problems.	علی: میری آنکھ، گلہ، پیٹ، منہ اور پورے جسم میں مسئلہ ہے	عالی: وہ دا ین چینگ سنگزی، دوزی، ذوی خاچھوآن شن یو وین تی۔	Ali: Mera ankh,gala, pet,munh, aur pure jism me masla hai.
大夫：你吃什么了？	Dàifū: Nǐ chī shénmele?	Doctor: What did you eat?	ڈاکٹر: آپ نے کیا کھایا تھا؟	دایفو: نی ٹھر شین می لہ؟	Doctor: Apne kiya khaya tah?
阿里：我挤不出来。	Ālǐ: Wǒ jǐ bù chūlái.	Ali: I do not remember.	علی: مجھے یاد نہیں	عالی: وہ چی بو ٹھو لاے۔	Ali: Mujhe Yad nahee.
大夫：好了,你学要打针，吃点药，休息几天就好了。	Dàifū: Hǎole, nǐ xué yào dǎzhēn, chī diǎn yào, xiūxí jǐ tiān jiù hǎole.	Doctor: Okay. You need injections. Eat some medicine, rest a few days, it will be all right.	ڈاکٹر: ٹھیک۔ آپ کو انجکشن کی ضرورت ہے۔ دوائی کھائیں، چند دن آرام کریں، پھر ٹھیک ہو جاے گا	دایفو: خاولا، نی شوی یاو ٹاٹرین، چی دیان یاو، شیوشی چی تیان چیو خاولا۔	Doctor: Theek ap ko injection ki zaroorat hai. Kuch dawa khaein Phir theek hojaega.

Lesson-86

Travelling – سیاحت Lūxíng, 旅行 Siyahat

Chinese	Pinyin	English	اُردو	چینی تلفظ	Roman Urdu
您什么时候去中国？	Nín shénme shíhou qù zhōngguó?	When will you go to China?	آپ کب چین جائیں گے؟	نین شینما شی ہو چھوی چو نگو آ ؟	Aap kab Cheen jae'nge?
我要下个月去哪里。	Wǒ yào xià gè yuè qù nàlǐ.	I will go there next month.	میں آءندہ ماہ وہاں جاوں گا	وو یاو شیا گہ یوے چھوی نالی۔	Mein aenda mah waha'n jaoo'n ga.
您在北京待几天？	Nín zài běijīng dài jǐ tiān?	How many days will you stay in Beijing?	آپ بیجنگ میں کتنے دن ٹھہریں گے؟	نین ذاے پیجنگ تاے چی تھیان؟	Aap Beijing me kitne deen thah'rein ge?
我要带一个星期。	Wǒ yào dài yīgè xīngqí.	I am going to stay for one week.	میں ایک ہفتہ رہوں گا	وہ یاو تاے ای گا شنگ چھی۔	Mein ek hafta ra-hoon ga.

Chinese	Pinyin	English	اُردو	چینی تلفظ	Roman Urdu
您要去哪些地方在北京？	Nín yào qù nǎxiē dìfāng zài běijīng?	Which places would you visit in Beijing?	آپ بیجنگ میں کونسی جگہیں جائیں گے ؟	نین یاو چھوی نای شے تی فانگ زای پیجنگ ؟	Aap Beijing me konsi jaghein jae'nge
我要去故宫，颐和园和长城。	Wǒ yào qù gùgōng, yíhéyuán hé chángchéng.	I will go to Palace Museum, Summer Palace and Great Wall.	میں پیلیس میوزیم، سمر پیلیس اور دیوار چین جاوں گا	ویاو چھوی کو کونگ، ایخایو آن خا ٹھانگ ٹھنگ	Mein Palace Museum, Summer Palace aur Deewar Cheen jaoo'nga.
北京名胜古迹很多。	Běijīng míngshèng gǔjī hěnduō.	Beijing has many famous places.	بیجنگ میں مشہور مقامات بہت ہیں	پیجنگ مینگ شنگ کو چی خین توو۔	Beijing me mashoor muqama'at bahut hein.

Lesson-87

Travelling– سیاحت Lūxíng, 旅行 Siyahat

Chinese	Pinyin	English	اُردو	چینی تلفظ	Roman Urdu
您是什么时候来巴基斯坦？	Nín shì shénme shíhou lái bājīsītǎn?	When did you come to Pakistan?	آپ پاکستان کب آئے؟	نین شی شینما شِ ہو لای پاچھستان؟	Aap Paki-stan kab aye?
您在巴基斯坦多久了？	Nín zài bājīsītǎn duōjiǔle?	How many days have you been in Paki-stan?	آپ کے پاکستان میں کتنے دن ہوے ہیں؟	نین ذای پاچھستان چی تھیان لہ؟	Aap ke Pa-kistan me kitne deen huy hein?
我在巴基斯坦一个星期了。	Wǒ zài bājīsītǎn yīgè xīngq-íle.	I have been in Pakistan for one week.	میں پاکستان میں ایک ہفتہ سے ہوں	وو ذای پاچھستان ایگا شین چھی لہ۔	Mein Pa-kistan me ek hafte se hoon.
你去哪些城市？	Nǐ qù nǎxiē chéngshì?	Which cities have you visited?	آپ کون سے شہر گئے ہیں؟	نی چھوی نا شی اے ٹھنگ شِی؟	Aap kon se shahr gaye hein?

Chinese	Pinyin	English	اُردو	چینی تلفظ	Roman Urdu
我去卡拉奇，拉合尔和伊斯兰堡。	Wǒ qù kǎlāqí, lā hé ěr hé yīsīlán-bǎo.	I went to Karachi, Lahore and Is-lamabad.	میں کراچی، لاہور اور اسلام آباد گیا	وچھوی کھالاچی لاخو آرخا اِسلان پاو۔	Mein Karachi, Lahore aur Islamabad gaya.
您感觉怎么样？	Nín gǎnjué zěnme yàng?	How did you feel?	آپ کو کیسا محسوس ہوا؟	نی کان چوے زین مایانگ؟	Aap ko kai-sa mahsus hua?
卡拉奇很大，拉合尔历史性和伊斯兰堡美丽城市。	Kǎlāqí hěn dà, lā hé ěr lìshǐ xìng hé yīsīlánbǎo měilì chéng-shì.	Karachi is big, Lahore is historic and Is-lamabad a beauti-ful city.	کراچی بڑا، لاہور تاریخی اور اسلام آباد خوبصورت شہر ہیں	کھا لا چی خین تا، لا خو آر لی شِ شنگ خا اسلان پاو میلی ٹھنگ شِی۔	Karachi barra,La-hore ta-reekhi aur Islamaba khubsurat shahar hein.

Lesson-88

Reception– ضیافت Zhāodàihuì, 招待会 Ziyafat

Chinese	Pinyin	English	اُردو	چینی تلفظ	Roman Urdu
我们打使今天邀请我们。	Wǒmen dǎ shǐ jīntiān yāoqǐng wǒmen.	Our ambassador has invited us to-day.	ہمارے سفیر صاحب نے آج ہمیں دعوت دی ہے	ومین تا شِی چِنتھیان یاو چھنگ ومین	HamareSafir Saheb ne aj hame dawat di hai.
今天是星期日。	Jīntiān shì xīngqírì.	Today is Sunday.	آج اتوار ہے	چِن تھیان شی سِنگھچی ری	Aaj Itwar hai.
今天我们又招待会。	Jīntiān wǒmen yòu zhāodài huì.	Today, we have a reception.	آج ہمارے ہاں ضیافت ہے۔	چِن تھیان ومین یاو چاو تاے خوئی	Aaj hamare ha'an ziyafat hai.
今天晚上我的朋友来。	Jīntiān wǎnshàng wǒ de péngyǒu lái.	Today evening, my friends will come.	آج شام میرے دوست آئیں گے	چِن تھیان وآن شَنگ و دا پھانگ یو لاے	Aaj sha'a Mere dost ayein ge.

Chinese	Pinyin	English	اُردو	چینی تلفظ	Roman Urdu
我和阿里是好朋友。	Wǒ hé ālǐ shì hǎo péngyǒu.	I and Ali are good friends.	میں اور علی اچھے دوست ہیں	وخا علی خاو پھانگ یو	Mein aur Ali ache dost hein.
阿里七点半会来。	Ālǐ qī diǎn bàn huì lái.	Ali will come at 7.30 o'clock.	علی ساڑھے سات بجے آے گا	عالی لاے چِھی تِیان پان	Ali sar'rh sa'at baje aye ga.
招待会八点开始。	Zhāodài huì bā diǎn kāishǐ.	The reception will start at 8 o'clock.	ضیافت کا آغاز آٹھ بجے ہو گا	چاوتاے خوئی پا تیان کھاءِشی	Ziyafat ka aghaz aa'th baje hoga
招待会结束九点。	Zhāodài huì jiéshù jiǔ diǎn.	The reception will end at 9 o'clock.	ضیافت نو بجے ختم ہو گا	چاو تاے خوئی چے شُو چیو تیان	Ziyafat no baje khatam hoga.

Lesson-89

Restaurant– ریستورآن Fànguǎn, 饭馆 Resturan

Chinese	Pinyin	English	اُردو	چینی تلفظ	Roman Urdu
您要去哪？	Nín yào qù nǎ?	Where are you going?	آپ کہاں جا رہے ہیں؟	نی یاو چھوئی نآر	Aap kahan jarahe hein?
我饿了	Wǒ èle	I am hungry.	مجھے بھوک لگ رہی ہے	وٴی لہ	Mujhe bhuuk lag rahee hai.
我要去饭馆	Wǒ yào qù fànguǎn	I want to go to restaurant.	میں ریستوران جانا چاہتا ہوں	ویاو چھوئی فن کو آن	Mein resturan ja'ana chahta hoon

Chinese	Pinyin	English	اُردو	چینی تلفظ	Roman Urdu
北京有很多清真饭馆	Běijīng yǒu hěnduō qīngzhēn fànguǎn	Beijing has many Muslim restau-rants.	بیجنگ میں بہت حلال ریستوران ہیں	پیجنگ یو خین ٹُو و چھینگ ٹرین فن کو آن	Beijing me bahut Halal resturan hein.
我喜欢吨各类顺河红兵楼	Wǒ xǐhuan dūn gè lèi shùn hé hóng bīng lóu	I like Dun-gleishun and Hong-binlou.	مجھے تونگ لائی شوءن اور خونگ پنگ لاو پسند ہیں	وشی خو آن تونگ لائی شوءن خا خونگ پینگ لاؤ	Mujhe Don-gleishun aur Hong binglou pasand hein.
他们从西单很近	Tāmen cóng xidān hěn jìn	They are very near from Xidan.	یہ دونوں شِی دان سے بہت قریب ہیں	تھامین صونگ شیدان خین چِن	Yeh dono Shi'dan se bahut qa-reeb hein.
我很喜欢中国菜	Wǒ hěn xǐhuan zhōngguó cài	I like Chinese food very much.	مجھے چینی کھانے بہت پسند ہیں	وخین شِی خو آن چونگو آصائی	Mujhe cheeni khane bahut pas-and hein.
中国在很好吃	Zhōngguó zài hěn hào chī	Chinese food is very deli-cious.	چینی کھانے بہت لذیذ ہیں	چونگو آ صائی خین خاو ٹھِی	Cheeni khane bahut lazeez hein.

Lesson-90

Dialogue between friends– دوستوں میں مکالمہ Liáotiān，聊天 Dosto mein mukalma

Chinese	Pinyin	English	اُردو	چینی تلفظ	Roman Urdu
李：阿里，您设么时候来北京？	Li: Ālǐ, nín shè me shíhou lái běijīng?	Li: Ali, when did you come to Beijing?	لی: علی آپ کب بیجنگ تشریف لائے؟	لی: نِی شینما شی ہو لائی بیجنگ	Li: Ali Aap kab Beijing tashrif laye?
阿里：我前天来北京。	Ālǐ: Wǒ qiántiān lái běijīng.	Ali: I came to Beijing yesterday.	علی: میں بیجنگ پرسوں آیا ہوں	علی: وچھیان تھِیان لائے بیجنگ	Ali: Mein Beijing parso'n aya hoon.
李：你在北京呆几天？	Li: Nǐ zài běijīng dāi jǐ tiān?	How many days you will stay in Beijing?	لی: آپ بیجنگ میں کتنے دن قیام کریں گے؟	لی: نِی ذائے بیجنگ تائی چی تھیان	Li: Aap Beijing me kitne deen qiyam ka-rein ge?
阿里，我在北京要呆一个礼拜	Ālǐ, wǒ zài běijīng yào dāi yīgè lǐbài	I wish to stay for a week in Beijing.	علی: میں بیجنگ میں ایک ہفتہ قیام کروں گا	علی: و ذائے بیجنگ یاو تائے اِیگا لی پائے	Ali: Mei Beijing Me ek hafta qiyam ka-roon ga.

Chinese	Pinyin	English	اُردو	چینی تلفظ	Roman Urdu
李：我祝您生活愉快。	Li: Wǒ zhù nín shēnghuó yúkuài.	I wish you happy stay.	لی: مجھے اُمید ہے آپ کا قیام اچھا گزرے گا	لی: و چھونِی شنگ خوو اِیوی کُھوآئی	Mujhe umeed hai aap ka qiyam acha guzre ga.
中国很漂亮	Zhōngguó hěn piào-liang	China is very beau-tiful.	چین بہت خوبصورت ہے	چونگو آ خین پھیاو لیانگ	Cheen bahut khubsurat hai.

Lesson-91

Dialogue between friends – دوستوں میں مکالمہ Liáotiān，聊天 Doston me mukalma

Chinese	Pinyin	English	اُردو	چینی تلفظ	Roman Urdu
阿亦莎：美林您设么时候来巴基斯坦？	Ā yì shā: Měi lín nín shè me shíhou lái bājīsītǎn?	Ayesha: Meilin, when did you arrive in Pakistan?	عائشہ: مے لِن آپ پاکستان کب پہنچیں؟	عائشہ: مے لن نِی شینما شِی ہو لائی پاچستھان	Ayesha Meilin aap kab Pakistan pahunche'en?
美林：我昨天来巴基斯坦	Měi lín: Wǒ zuótiān lái bājīsītǎn	Meilin: I came to Pakistan yesterday.	مے لن: میں کل پاکستان پہنچی ہوں	مے لین: وو تھیان لائی پاچستھان	Meilin: Mein kal Pakistan pahunchi hoon.
阿亦莎：你在巴基斯坦呆几天	Ā yì shā: Nǐ zài bājīsītǎn dāi jǐ tiān	Ayesha: How many days, will you stay in Pakistan?	عائشہ: آپ پاکستان میں کتنے دن قیام کریں گی؟	عائشہ: نِی ذاے پاچستھان تائی چی تھیان	Ayesha: Pakistan me kitne deen qiyam karein gi?

Chinese	Pinyin	English	اُردو	چینی تلفظ	Roman Urdu
美林：巴基斯坦则么样？	Měi lín: Bājīsītǎn zé me yàng?	Meilin: How is Pakistan?	مے لِن: پاکستان کیسا ہے؟	مے لِن: پاچستھان ذیما یانگ	Meilin: Pakistan kaisa hai?
美林：巴基斯坦很漂亮	Měi lín: Bājīsītǎn hěn piàoliang	Meilin: Pakistan is very beautiful.	مے لِن: پاکستان بہت خوبصورت ہے	مے لِن: پاچستھان خین پھیاو لیانگ	Meilin: Pakistan bahut khubsurat hai.

Lesson-92

Affirmative Sentences – اقراری جملے Kěn jùzi, 肯句子 Iqrari jumle

Chinese	Pinyin	English	اُردو	چینی تلفظ	Roman Urdu
我是哈桑	Wǒ shì hā sān	I am Hasan.	میں حسن ہوں	وشی حسن	Mein Hasan hoon.
我是巴基斯坦人	Wǒ shì bājīsītǎn rén	I am Pakistani.	میں پاکستانی ہوں	وشی پاچستھان رین	Mein Pakistani hoon.
我照李老师	Wǒ zhào li lǎoshī	I am looking for Teacher Li.	میں استاد لی کو ڈھونڈ رہا ہوں	وچاو لی لاو شی	Mein Ustad Li ko dhu'nd raha hoon.
我要学韩语	Wǒ yào xué hán yǔ	I wish to study Chinese.	میں چینی زبان پڑھنا چاہتا ہوں	و یاو شوے خانوی	Mein Cheeni zaban par'rhna Chahta hoon.
我昨天来的	Wǒ zuótiān lái de	I came yesterday.	میں کل آیا ہوں	وذو تھیان لائی دا	Mein kal a'ya hoon.

Lesson-93

Affirmative Sentences – اقراری جملے Kěn jùzi, 肯句子 Iqrari jumle

Chinese	Pinyin	English	اُردو	چینی تلفظ	Roman Urdu
我是从巴基斯坦来的	Wǒ shì cóng bājīsītǎn lái de	I have come from Pakistan.	میں پاکستان سے آیا ہوں	وشی سونگ پاچستھان لاے	Mein Paki-stan se a'ya hoon.
我喜欢学汉语	Wǒ xǐhuan xué hànyǔ	I would like to study Chinese.	میں چینی زبان پڑھنا چاہتا ہوں	وشی خوآن شوے خانوی	Mein Cheeni par'rhna chahta hoon.
我要到北京语言文化大学去	Wǒ yào dào běijīng yǔyán wénhuà dàxué qù	I would like to go to Beijing Languag-es and Culture University.	میں بیجنگ کے جامعہ زبان و ثقافت جانا چاہتا ہوں	و یاو تاو پیجنگ ایوی یان وینخو آتاشوے چھوئی	Mein Beijing ke Jame'a Zaban wo saqafat jana chahta hoon.
我吃饱了	Wǒ chī bǎole	I have eaten my food.	میں نے کھانا کھا لیا ہے	وٹھر پاو لا	Mein ne khana kha liya hai.
我要睡觉	Wǒ yào shuìjiào	I want to sleep.	میں سونا چاہتا ہوں	ویاو شوئی چیاو	Mein sona chahta hoon.
我要读书	Wǒ yào dúshū	I want to read.	میں پڑھنا چاہتا ہوں	ویاو تو شو	Mein par'rhna Chahta hoon.

Lesson-94

Negative Sentences – منفی جملے Fǒu jùzi，否句子 Munfi jumle

Chinese	Pinyin	English	اُردو	چینی تلفظ	Roman Urdu
他不是我的老师	Tā bùshì wǒ de lǎoshī	He is not my teacher.	وہ میرا اُستاد نہیں ہے	تھا پُو شِی ودا لاو شِی	Woh mera Ustad nahee hai.
你们不是学生	Nǐmen bùshì xuéshēng	You (plural) are not students.	آپ لوگ طالب علم نہیں ہیں	نِی مین پو شِی شُوے شنگ	Aap log talib ilm nahee hein.
我的朋友不是他	Wǒ de péngyǒu bùshì tā	He/she is not my friend.	وہ میرا دوست نہیں ہے	و دا پھانگ یو پو شِی تھا	Who mera dost nahee hai.
那个人不是我的同学	Nàgè rén bùshì wǒ de tóngxué	He is not my classmate.	وہ میرا کلاس فیلو نہیں ہے	نیگا رین پو شِی و دا تھونگ شُوے	Who mera class fellow nahee hai.
这个女人我不认识	Zhège nǚrén wǒ bù rènshi	I do not know this lady.	میں اِس خاتون کو نہیں پہنچانتا ہوں	چیگا نِوی رین و پو رین شِی	Mein is khatoon ko nahee pachanta hoon.

Lesson-95

Interrogative Sentences – سوالیہ جملے Wèn jùzi，问句子 Sawaliya Jumle

Chinese	Pinyin	English	اُردو	چینی تلفظ	Roman Urdu
您是谁	Nín shì shuí	Who are you?	آپ کون ہیں؟	نی شی شُوی؟	Aap kon hein?
您是哪里人	Nín shì nǎlǐ rén	Where are you from?	آپ کہاں کے رہنے والے ہیں؟	نِی شی نالی رین؟	Aap kahan ke rahne wale hein
您找谁	Nín zhǎo shuí	Whom do you want to meet?	آپ کسے تلاش کر رہے ہیں؟	نِی چاو شوی؟	Aap kise talash kar-rahe hein?
您要社么	Nín yào shè me	What do you want?	آپ کو کیا چاہیے؟	نِی یاو شین ما؟	Aap ko kiya chah'ye?
您设么时候来	Nín shè me shíhou lái	What time did you come?	آپ کس وقت آئے؟	نِی شین ما شی ہو لائے؟	Aap kis waqt a'ye?

Lesson-96

Interrogative Sentences – سوالیہ جملے Wèn jùzi，问句子 Sawaliya Jumle

Chinese	Pinyin	English	اُردو	چینی تلفظ	Roman Urdu
您从哪来	Nín cóng nă lái	Where did you come from?	آپ کہاں سے تشریف لائے؟	نِی صونگ نار لائے؟	Aap kahan se tashreef la'ye?
您喜欢社么	Nín xǐhuan shè me	What do you like?	آپ کیا پسند کرتے ہیں؟	نِی شی خوآن شین ما؟	Aap kiya pasand karte hein?
您要到哪儿去	Nín yào dào nă'er qù	Where would you like to go?	آپ کہاں جانا پسند کریں گے؟	نِی یاو تاو نار چھوی؟	Aap kahan jana pas-and karein ge?
您吃饭了吗	Nín chīfàn-le ma	Have you eaten?	آپ نے کھانا کھا لیا ہے؟	نِی ٹھی فن لا ما؟	Aap ne khana kha liya hai?
您要睡觉吗	Nín yào shuìjiào ma	Do you want to sleep?	آپ سونا چاہتے ہیں؟	نِی یاو شوئی چیاو ما؟	Aap sona chahte hein?

Chinese	Pinyin	English	اُردو	چینی تلفظ	Roman Urdu
他是谁	Tā shì shuí	Who is he/ she?	وہ کون ہے؟	تھا شی شوی؟	Who kon hai?
您们是谁	Nínmen shì shuí	Who are you? (plural)	آپ لوگ کون ہیں؟	نِی مین شی شوی؟	Aap log kon hein?
您的朋友是谁	Nín de péngyǒu shì shuí	Who is your friend?	آپ کا دوست کون ہے؟	نِی دا پھانگ یو شی شوی؟	Aap ka dost kon hai?
那个人是谁	Nàgè rén shì shuí	Who is that man?	وہ آدمی کون ہے؟	نیگا رین شی شوی؟	Who a'admi Kon hai?
这个女人是谁	Zhège nǚrén shì shuí	Who is this woman?	یہ عورت کون ہے؟	چیگا نِوی رین شی شوی؟	Yeh aurat kon hai?

Lesson-97

Interrogative Sentences – سوالیہ جملے Wèn jùzi，问句子 Sawaliya Jumle

Chinese	Pinyin	English	اُردو	چینی تلفظ	Roman Urdu
那个孩子是谁	Nàgè háizi shì shuí	Who is that child?	وہ بچہ کون ہے؟	نیگا ہاءزہ شی شوی؟	Who bacha kon hai?
谁知道我来中国	Shuí zhīdào wǒ lái zhōngguó	Who knew, I will come to China?	کسے پتہ تھا کہ میں چین آوں گا؟	شوئی چِی تاو و لائی چونگوآ؟	Kise pata tah Ke mein Cheen aoon ga?
您从哪个国家来	Nín cóng nǎge guójiā lái	Which country you come from?	آپ کس ملک سے تشریف لاے ہیں؟	نِی صونگ نیگا کو چیالاے؟	Aap kis mulk se tashreef laye hein?
他是哪国人	Tā shì nǎ guórén	Which country he comes from?	وہ کس ملک کا باشندہ ہے؟	تھا شی نا گو آرین؟	Who kis mulk ka bashinda hai?
阿力邀去哪个国家	Ā lì yāo qù nǎge guójiā	Which country Ali wants to go?	علی کون سے ملک جانا چاہتا ہے؟	علی یاوچھوی نیگا کوچیا؟	Ali kon se mulk jana chahta hai?

Chinese	Pinyin	English	اُردو	چینی تلفظ	Roman Urdu
他喜欢哪个	Tā xǐhuan nǎge	Which one he/she likes?	اُسے کون والا پسند ہے؟	تھا شی خوان نیگا؟	U'se kon wala pas-and hai?
您的朋友是哪个人	Nín de péngyǒu shì nǎge rén	Who is your friend?	آپ کا دوست کون ہے؟	نِی دا پھانگ یو شِی نیگا رین؟	Aap ka dost kon hai?

Lesson-98

One Family – ایک خاندان yījiā rén, 一家人 Ek khan'daan

Chinese	Pinyin	English	اُردو	چینی تلفظ	Roman Urdu
中国和巴基斯坦是一家人	Zhōngguó hé bā-jīsītǎn shì yījiā rén	China and Pakistan are one family.	چین اور پاکستان کے لوگ ایک خاندان کی طرح ہیں	چُونگو آ خا پاچستھان اِی چیارین	Cheen aur Pakistan ke log ek khandaa-n ki tarah hein.
中国人热爱巴基斯坦人	Zhōngguó rén rè'ài bājīsītǎn rén	Chinese people deeply love Pakistani people.	چین کے لوگ پاکستان کے عوام سے دل کی گہرائیوں سے محبت کرتے ہیں	چونگو آ رین رآ آئی، پاچستھان رین	Cheen ke log Pakistan se dil ki gahrayo'n se muhabbat Karte hein.
中国和巴基斯坦互相帮助	Zhōng-guó hé bājīsītǎn hùxiāng bāngzhù	China and Pakistan help each other.	چین اور پاکستان ایک دوسرے کی مدد کرتے ہیں	چونگو آ خا پاچستھان خو شیانگ پانگ چُو	Cheen aur Pa-kistan ek dusre ki madad karte hein.

Chinese	Pinyin	English	اُردو	چینی تلفظ	Roman Urdu
中国和巴基斯坦好朋友，好兄弟，好邻居，好伙伴。	Zhōngguó hé bā-jīsītǎn hǎo péngyǒu, hǎo xiōng-dì, hǎo línjū, hǎo huǒbàn.	China and Pakistan are good friends, good brothers, good neighbours and good partners.	چین اور پاکستان اچھے دوست، اچھے بھائی، اچھے پڑوسی اور اچھے ساتھی ہیں	چونگوآ، خا پاچستھان خاو پھانگ یو، خاو شینگ تِی خاو لینگ چوئی، خاو خُوپان	Cheen aur Pa-kistan ach'che dost,ach'che bhai, ach'che par'rosi aur ach'che sa'athi hein.

Lesson-99

Expressing Gratitude: اظہار تشکر Biǎoshì gǎnxiè, 表示感谢 Izhar tashakur

Chinese	Pinyin	English	اُردو	چینی تلفظ	Roman Urdu
感谢	gǎnxiè	grateful	مشکور	کان شیے	Shukriya
非常感谢	Fēicháng gǎnxiè	Many thanks	بہت بہت شکریہ	فے تھانگ کان شیے	Bahut bahut shukriya
谢谢您	Xièxiè nín	Grateful to you	آپ کا شکریہ	شیے شیے نِین	Aap ka shukriya.
太感谢您	Tài gǎnxiè nín	Lot of thanks to you	آپ کا بہت بہت شکریہ	تھائی کان شیے نِین	Aap ka ba-hut bahut shukriya
多谢您	Duōxiè nín	Many thanks to you	آپ کا بہت شکریہ	تُوو شیے نِین	Aap ka bahut shukriya.
麻烦您了	Máfan nínle	Bothered you	آپ کو زحمت دی	مافین نین لا	Aap ko zah-mat diya.
对不起	Duìbùqǐ	Excuse me	معاف کیجیے	تُوئی پُوچھی	Mua'af Kijye.
我要向你们学习	Wǒ yào xiàng nǐmen xuéxí	I want to learn from you (plural)	میں آپ لوگوں سے سیکھنا چاہتاہوں	وو یاو شیانگ نی مین شُوے شِی	Mein aap logon se seekhna chahta hoon.
巴中友谊万岁	Ba zhōng yǒuyì wànsuì	Long live Pak-China Friendship	پاک چین دوستی زندہ باد	پاچونگ یو اِی وآن سوئی	Pak Cheeni dosti zind-abad

Lesson-100

Felicitations – مبارکباد Zhùhè, 祝贺 Mubarak baad

Chinese	Pinyin	English	اُردو	چینی تلفظ	Roman Urdu
生日快乐	Shēngrì kuàilè	Happy Birth-day	سالگرہ مبارک	چونی شنگری کھواءلا	Salgirah-Mubarak!
新年快乐	Xīnnián kuàilè	Happy New Year	نیا سال مبارک	شینیان کھواءلا	Naya sal Mubarak!
春节愉快	Chūnjié yúkuài	Happy Spring Fes-tival	موسم بہاراں مبارک	ایوی کھوآئی دا ٹھوءن چے	Mausim Baharan Mubarak!
祝你发财，长寿和繁荣	Zhù nǐ fācái, chángshòu hé fánróng	I wish you fortune, longevity and pros-perity	آپ کو دولت، دراز عمر اور خوشی عطا ہو	چونی چیشیانگ، ٹھانگشوخافان رونگ	Aap ko daulat, daraz umar aur khushi ata'a ho!
祝愿中国一个繁荣和光明的未来	Zhùyuàn zhōngguó yīgè fánróng hé guāng-míng de wèilái	I wish Chi-na a prosperous and bright future	چین کو خوشحالی اور درخشاں مستقبل عطاہو	شی وآنگ وے چونگوآ دا فانرونگ خاکوانگ مینگ دا ویلاے	Cheen ko khush-hali,da-rakhshan mustaqbil ata'a ho!
祝愿巴中友谊将有光明的未来	Zhùyuàn ba zhōng yǒuyì jiāng yǒu guāngmíng de wèilái	I wish Paki-stan-China friendship a bright future	پاک چین دوستی کو روشن مستقبل عطا ہو۔	شی وآنگ پاچونگ یُوای کُوانگ داویلاے	Pak Cheen dosti ko roshan mus-taqbil ata'a ho!

Pearls of Chinese Wisdom

چینی حکمت کے زرین اصول

English	اُردو
Humility earns greatness	انکساری و عاجزی بُلند جاتی ہے
Good temper wins friends	اچھے مزاج والوں کے دوست زیادہ ہوتے ہیں
Respect is earned, not inherited	عزت ورثہ میں نہیں بلکہ محبت سے حاصل ہوتی ہے
Blindly copying others can be disastrous	اندھی تقلید سے نقصان ہوتا ہے
No body leaves the place, where he is fed	کوئی آسودگی کی جگہ نہیں چھوڑتا
Best Judgment is only possible after hearing both sides	صحیح فیصلہ دونوں جانب کی رائے لے کر ہی ممکن ہے
A human being knows himself more than others do	ہر آدمی خودشناسی جانتا ہے
The seeking of knowledge never ends	علم کی جستجو کبھی ختم نہیں ہو سکتی
Happiness is never far	خوشی زیادہ دور نہیں ہوتی ہے
Even rubbish has a material value	کوئی شے بے کار نہیں ہوتی ہے

English	اُردو
Unintended actions bring unintended consequences	غیر دانستہ اعمال کے نتائج بھی غیر دانستہ ہی ہوتے ہیں
Those who are determined are blessed with divine help	مصمم ارادے رکھنے والوں کو روحانی مدد بھی ہوتی ہے
One suffers for one's actions and inactions	ہر شخص کو اپنے عمل اور غیر عمل کی وجہ پر بھگتنا پڑتا ہے
Merit promotes strength	قابلیت ، صلاحیت سے طاقت میں اضافہ ہوتا ہے
Love begets love	محبت سے محبت بڑھتی ہے
A good sleep is better than a good meal	اچھی نیند اچھی غذا سے بہتر ہے
Time tests friendship	پائیدار دوستی وقت کی محتاج ہوتی ہے
Trust is never built in one deep meeting	اعتماد ایک ملاقات میں نہیں بنتا ہے
Self awareness is the most precious gift	خودی سب سے بہترین تحفہ ہے
Every human being has two opportunities in life.	ہر شخص کو زندگی میں دو مرتبہ مواقع آتے ہیں
Every challenge is a potential opportunity.	ہر مشکل ایک موقع بھی فراہم کرتی ہے
Societies change every thirty years	معاشرہ ہر تیس سال میں تبدیل ہوتا ہے
Faith saves life	ایمان زندگی بچاتا ہے
No person is born without talent	کوئی آدمی بغیر صلاحیت کے پیدا نہیں ہوتا ہے

English	اُردو
The ultimate truth has several explanations.	سچائی کے کئی پہلو ہوتے ہیں
Better the teacher, better the students.	بہتر استاد، بہتر طالب علم
Vegetables do not taste like meat/mutton.	سبزی میں گوشت کا مزہ نہیں ہو سکتا۔
Preparing for exam is more difficult than giving birth	امتحان دینا بچہ پیدا کرنے سے زیادہ مشکل کام ہے۔
Truth can never be hidden.	حقیقت چھپائی نہیں جا سکتی
Hypocrisy is a self defeating act.	چاپلوسی کو شکست ہوتی ہے
Fools loose every thing	بیوقوف سب کچھ کھو دیتا ہے
Poor memory leads to loss in judgement.	یاداشت کی کمی قوت فیصلہ متاثر کرتی ہے
Extra ordinary problems need extra ordinary solutions.	غیر معمولی مسائل کے لیے غیر معمولی حل ضروری ہوتے ہیں
Even angels fear bullies	فرشتے بھی بدمعاش سے پناہ مانگتے ہیں
Jealousy knows no limit.	حسد کی کوئی حد نہیں ہوتی ہے
The official follows the rule	سرکاری ملازم لکیر کا فقیر ہوتا ہے۔
Happiness in home but searching for it outside	گھر میں خوشی لیکن تلاش باہر
Searching for measurement, when one's feet are there	پیر موجود لیکن ناپ کی تلاش

English	اُردو
Every person is responsible for his own demise	ہر انسان اپنی تباہی کاخود ذمہ دار ہوتا ہے
Poetry is reflective of deep emotions	شاعری گہرے جذبات کی عکاسی ہوتی ہے
Big promises are short in implementation	جس قدر اچھے وعدے، اُس قدر کم اُمید عمل کا ہو گا
Putting official's hat on monk's head does not make him official	بابو کی ٹوپی پیر کے سر پر ڈالنے سے بابو نہیں بنتا
Indulgence in mental exercise does not satisfy one's hunger	ذہنی عیاشی سے پیٹ نہیں بھرتا
Quarrelsome people find every excuse	جھگڑالو کے لیے بہانہ ہی کافی ہے
The corrupt are devious	بد عنوانوں کے ہزار راستے ہوتے ہیں
Only the father knows, what the son feels	صرف باپ کو بیٹے کا احساس ہوتا ہے
The dwarf serves his life by his intelligence	بونے کی زندگی ذہانت سے بچتی ہے
The crooks have no principles	بد قماشوں کے کوئی اصول نہیں ہوتے
Cooking the goose without catching it	خواب میں مرغ کا سالن بنانا بیکار ہے
Pain in the arm but caring for the robe	ہاتھ میں زخم لیکن پوشاک کی فکر

English	اُردو
Bad luck knows no seasons	بد قسمتی کسی موسم کا محتاج نہیں
Storm in the ocean but cries at home	طوفان سمندر میں لیکن ماتم گھر میں
Breaking the tea set for cooking the turtle	کچھوے کو پکانے کے لیے چائے دانی کو توڑنا
Idiots do not grow wise with age	احمق ہمیشہ احمق ہی رہتا ہے
Horse in the house but searching for it outside	گھوڑا گھر میں لیکن تلاش باہر
Happiness needs no colour description	خوشی کا اظہار کسی ایک رنگ کا محتاج نہیں
Soul searching while being drunk	اپنا حواس نہیں، روح کی تلاش
Invitation for one on behalf of ten	دعوت ایک کے لیے نام دس ہزار کا
Locusts (calamities) need no invitation	(مصیبت) ٹڈی دل کسی دعوت کی محتاج نہیں
Father's wealth makes the son incompetent	باپ کی دولت بیٹے کی نااہلی کی وجہ بن سکتی ہے
Enemy in the house, searching for the key outside	دشمن گھر میں، چابی کی تلاش باہر
Lacking eyesight but blaming the dog	خود بینائی نہیں لیکن کتے پر الزام

English	اُردو
Weak eyesight but blaming the bad stomach	آنکھ کی بینائی خراب، الزام پیٹ پر
Greatness also comes from genealogy	عظمت وراثت میں بھی ملتی ہے
Bride enjoys prime of husband's life	دلہن کو شوہر کے ابتدائی دن اچھے لگتے ہیں
Presence of mind saves one life	حاضر دماغی کسی کی جان بچا سکتی ہے
Morality is not the sole heritage of any one	اخلاقیات کسی شخص کی میراث نہیں
The son benefits from father's title	اولاد کو باپ کے عہدہ کا فائدہ ہوتا ہے
God helps those who have no one else to turn to	خدا اس کی مدد کرتا ہے جس کا کوئی نہیں ہوتا ہے
Patience is even more difficult than incurring debt	صبر کی گھڑیاں، قرض لینے سے زیادہ بھاری ہوتی ہے
The vagabond is happy with himself	درویش (مست) لوگ اپنے آپ سے خوش رہتے ہیں
A hungry man loses his self esteem	ایک بھوکا آدمی اپنی عزت نفس کھو بیٹھتا ہے
The debtor bows to get loans only while the creditor has to bow until he gets it back	قرض دار صرف قرض لیتے وقت جھکتا ہے جبکہ قرض دینے والوں کو واپس لینے تک جُھکا رہنا پڑتا ہے

English	اُردو
Failing to practice those virtues/principles that one preaches	اپنے اصول کی خود خلاف ورزی کرنا اور دوسروں کو عمل کی تلقین کرنا
The cat can never be a vegetarian	بلی کبھی سبزی خور نہیں ہو سکتی
A workaholic ultimately fails to recognize himself or his belongings	کسی کام کے جنونی کو آخرکار اپنی اور اپنے سامان کی شناخت نہیں ہوتی
The guest should not overstay his welcome	مہمان کو میزبان کی صبر کی حد کا خیال رکھنا چاہیے
The liar has hundred stories	جھوٹ بولنے والے کے پاس سو کہانیاں ہوتی ہیں
The devious live off the fool's earnings	بدمعاش بیوقوفوں کی کمائی پر گزارہ کرتا ہے
Being poor and fool means double calamity	غریب اور بیوقوف ہونا دوہری مصیبت ہے
Only those who are hollow within, talk big	جو اندر سے خالی ہوتا ہے، وہ بڑکیں زیادہ مارتا ہے
Most inventions / discoveries come by chance while the rest come out of necessity	زیادہ تر ایجادات اور دریافت اتفاقیہ ہوا کرتے ہیں جبکہ بقیہ ضرورت کی تحت
Laughter breeds laughter	ہنسنے کے لیے دوسروں کی ہنسی ہی کافی ہے
Even disabilities have advantages	اپاہج کی بھی اپنی شان ہے

English	اُردو
The great the scholar, the more detached from reality	جس قدر بڑا عالم، اس قدر حقیقت سے دور
It is useless to expect the ignorant to show the way	لاعلم سے رہنمائی کی اُمید بے سود ہے
Those who keep eyes closed can be even more dangerous	جو آنکھ بند رکھتے ہیں، وہ زیادہ خطرناک ہو سکتے ہیں
For the dying, it does not matter how they die	مرنے والوں کو پرواہ نہیں ہوتی کہ وہ کس طرح مر رہے ہیں
Good obituary require good deeds	اچھے کتبہ کے لیے عمل کا اچھا ہونا بھی ضروری ہے
Gentlemen keep silent	شریف لوگ خاموش رہتے ہیں
The corrupt never repents	بدعنوان کبھی توبہ نہیں کرتے ہیں
Excessive praise is often insincere	کسی حد سے زیادہ تعریف، بکواس ہی ہو سکتی ہے
Doctors do not write prescriptions for themselves	ڈاکٹر حضرات اپنے لیے نسخہ نہیں لکھتے
The miser do not wish to lose money even dying	کنجوس مرتے وقت بھی پیسہ چھوڑنا نہیں چاہتا
Some extravagance can be necessary	کچھ اسراف ضروری ہوتا ہے
Some form of treatment can cure the disease but kill the person	کچھ طریقہ علاج سے شفاع تو ممکن ہے لیکن مریض کا بچنا نہیں

English	اُردو
Officials with poor memory can give poor judgements	جن افسر صاحبان کی یاداشت ٹھیک نہیں، ان کے فیصلے غلط ہوتے ہیں
Even the most brave men remain silent in front of his wife	حتیٰ کہ بہادر لوگ بھی اپنی بیوی کے سامنے خاموش رہتے ہیں
Animals know no etiquette while beasts know no mercy	جانوروں کو مجلسی آداب نہیں پتہ جبکہ درندوں میں رحم کا فقدان ہوتا ہے
A mean person would remain so under all conditions	ایک کنجوس ہر حال میں کنجوس ہی رہتا ہے
Every person is a victim of his habits	ہر شخص اپنی عادت سے مجبور ہوتا ہے
One problem can breads another and eventually to a completely different issue	ایک مسئلہ سے دوسرا مسئلہ اور اس کے بعد اگلا مسئلہ بالکل مختلف انداز کا ہو سکتا ہے
Whatever you are doing, always have an escape route	آپ کچھ بھی کر رہے ہوں، راہ فرار ضرور ہوناچاہیے
People with lack of vision fall again and again	دوراندیشی سے محروم لوگ بار بار گرتے ہیں
Those who invent tools to hurt others may themselves become its victim	جو دوسروں کی تباہی کا راستہ کھولتے ہیں، وہ خود ہی شکار ہوجاتے ہیں

English	اُردو
Impartiality promotes merit	غیر جانبداری صلاحیت کو پروان چڑھاتی ہے
Borrowed fame is always short lived	اُدھار کی شہرت عارضی ہوتی ہے
Rumours destabilize and destroy	افواہ سے تباہی و بربادی ہوتی ہے
Near and dear ones can not judge themselves	عزیزو اقارب اپنے بارے میں صحیح راے نہیں دے سکتے
Achievement of target is dependent on direction	مقصد کا حصول صرف سمت کے تعین کے بعد ہی ممکن ہے
Keeping a promise makes one grow strong and prosperous	وعدہ کی پابندی مضبوطی اور خوشحالی لاتی ہے
Even a little talent, can be put to good use	زرّہ بھر صلاحیت کا بھی مفید استعمال ہوسکتا ہے
Constructive cristicism is necessary for improvement	تعمیری تنقید سے ہی بہتری ممکن ہے
What comes free, can not be forever.	مفت کا مال ہمیشہ نہیں رہ سکتا۔
Self awareness is the most precious thing	خودی سے آگاہی سب سے بڑی دولت ہے
The fools have ultimately themselves to hurt	احمق کو آخرکار خود ہی نقصان ہوتا ہے
The fools are short of common sense	احمق عقل سلیم سے بھی محروم ہوتا ہے

English	اُردو
It is easier to see other's faults than one's own.	بُرائی ہمیشہ دوسروں میں نظر آتی ہے
Curing an illness is possible only when done in time.	کسی بیماری کا علاج وقت گزارنے کے بعد ممکن نہیں
A successful business depens on its accessibility.	کسی کاروبار کی کامیابی اُس کی اپنی رسائی پر انحصار کرتی ہے
Life needs balancing act for success.	زندگی میں کامیابی کے لیے متوازن عمل ضروری ہے
Greed leads to destruction	لالچ کا نتیجہ تباہی کی صورت میں ہو تا ہے
Flattery reduces one's credibility	خوشامد انسان کی قدر گھٹاتی ہے
Hurting some one's dignity could hurt oneself.	کسی کی عزت نفس کو مجروح کرنے سے خود نقصان ہوتا ہے
Talk only, when it is useful	صرف مفید بات کرنی چاہیے
Committed people can move mountains by their sheer will.	ذمہ دار لوگ اپنی قوت اِرادی سے پہاڑ بھی ہٹا سکتے ہیں
Tragedies and tribulation affect sound judgement.	حادثے اور مصیبتیں انسان کی درست فیصلہ کی قوت متاثر کرتے ہیں۔
Even a noble act could have negative results.	کسی نیک عمل کا بھی منفی نتیجہ ہو سکتا ہے
Only hard work can earn prosperity.	صرف محنت سے ہی خوشحالی ممکن ہے۔
Everyone likes his own environment.	ہر کسی کو اپنا ماحول پسند ہے۔

English	اُردو
Everyone has his individuality in life.	ہر شخص زندگی میں اِنفرادیت رکھتا ہے۔
One timely help is worth more than a million promises.	ایک وقت پر مدد، لاکھوں وعدوں سے بہتر ہے۔
The Lure of gain is sure to bring pain.	لالچ بُری بلا ہے۔
The picture is not same as reality.	تصویر حقیقت کی طرح نہیں ہوتی ہے۔
Children's character is built by mother.	ماں بچے کا کردار بناتی ہے۔
Safety lies in unity.	اتفاق میں برکت ہے۔
Greed can cost life.	لالچ سے زندگی جاتی ہے۔
Everyone knows his own shortcomings.	ہر کسی کو اپنی کمزوری کا پتہ ہوتا ہے۔
A bully can not be appeased	غنڈہ کو کبھی خوش نہیں کیا جا سکتا۔
Every rascal has an excuse.	ہر بدمعاش کے پاس عُذر ہوتا ہے۔
Appearance does not change reality.	بھیس کسی حقیقت کو چھپا نہیں سکتی۔
Perseverance wins the goal.	ثابت قدمی سے مقصد کا حصول ممکن ہے۔

PAKISTAN – CHINA FRIENDSHIP

S.RABYA HASAN JAVED

Pakistan and China,

Both their friendship unbreakably strong,

Both their friendship unstoppably long,

Such a friendship, more valuable than gold,

All Pakistanis and Chinese, all the young and the old,

From the past, from the ages of our elder ones,

Such a friendship, such a truthful one stuns,

This friendship outstand any other, in front of our eyes,

So truthful, so strong, there are no lies,

For Pakistan and China friendship to live on, standing beside are

Us, me and you,

We see this friendship perfect itself, as I said truthful and strong,

It's all true!

This friendship, our elders have seen,

They know all; they know what it means,

Now it's our time, us young ones, you and me,

We have to learn a lot, many things we have to see,

China will always be our friend,

I know that, you know that, friends from beginning to no end!

Pk.chineseembassy.org/eng

Dated: 27/09/2009

巴中友谊

作者：拉比亚·哈桑·贾维德

两国友谊牢不可破
两国友谊源远流长
我们的友谊，比金子还珍贵
巴中两国人民，不论年老年少
从过去,到现在
我们的友谊，令世人称道
在我们眼里，巴中友谊高于一切。
巴中友谊，
如此真诚，如此牢固，
没有欺骗，没有谎言。
巴中友谊，
如此真诚，如此牢固，
成长背后，有我有你。
我们的祖辈是巴中友谊的证者，
他们知道，这样的友谊来之不易。
现在，轮到我们年轻人了。
你和我，
我们必须了解，必须铭记，
中国是我们永远的朋友。
我们相信，
巴中友谊，永无止境。

http://world.people.com.cn/GB/10128084.html
Dated: 27/09/2009

Ba zhōng yŏuyì

Zuòzhĕ: Lā bĭ yă•hā sāng•jiăwéidé

Liăng guó yŏuyì láobùkĕpò
Liăng guó yŏuyì yuányuănliúcháng
Wŏmen de yŏuyì, bĭ jīn zĭ huán zhēnguì
Ba zhōng liăng guó rénmín, bùlùn nián lăonián shào
Cóng guòqù dào xiànzài
Wŏmen de yŏuyì, lìng shìrén chēngdào
Zài wŏmen yăn lĭ, ba zhōng yŏuyì gāo yú yīqiè.
Ba zhōng yŏuyì,
Rúcĭ zhēnchéng, rúcĭ láogù,
Méiyŏu qīpiàn, méiyŏu huăngyán.
Ba zhōng yŏuyì,
Rúcĭ zhēnchéng, rúcĭ láogù,
Chéngzhăng bèihòu, yŏu wŏ yŏu nĭ.
Wŏmen de zŭbèi shì ba zhōng yŏuyì de zhèng zhĕ,
Tāmen zhīdào, zhèyàng de yŏuyì lái zhī bùyì.
Xiànzài, lún dào wŏmen niánqīng rénle.
Nĭ hé wŏ,
Wŏmen bìxū liăojiĕ, bìxū míngjì,
Zhōngguó shì wŏmen yŏngyuăn de péngyŏu.
Wŏmen xiāngxìn,
Ba zhōng yŏuyì, yŏng wú zhĭjìng.